The Hash Knife Brand

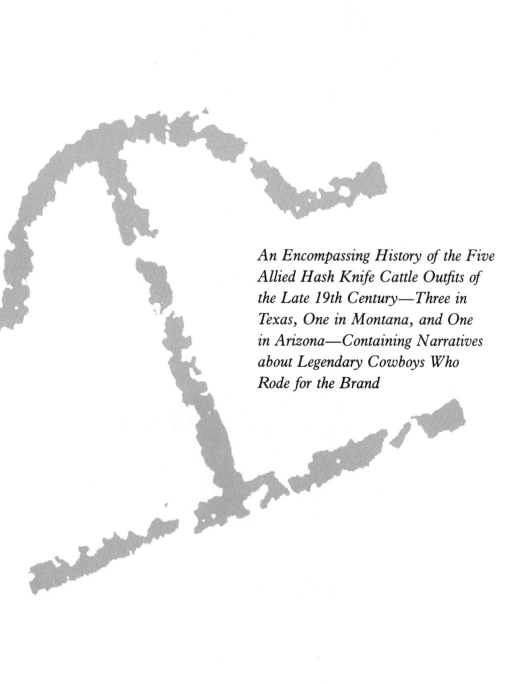

*An Encompassing History of the Five
Allied Hash Knife Cattle Outfits of
the Late 19th Century—Three in
Texas, One in Montana, and One
in Arizona—Containing Narratives
about Legendary Cowboys Who
Rode for the Brand*

The

Jim Bob Tinsley

University Press of Florida

Gainesville
Tallahassee
Tampa
Boca Raton
Pensacola
Orlando
Miami
Jacksonville

Library of Congress Cataloging in
Publication Data

Tinsley, Jim Bob.
The hash knife brand / Jim
Bob Tinsley.
p. cm.
Includes bibliographical
references and index.
ISBN 0–8130–1210–4.—ISBN
0–8130–1211–2 (pbk.)
1. Ranch life—Southwest,
New—History. 2. Hash Knife
Brand. 3. Cowboys—Southwest,
New—History. 4. Cattle trade—
Southwest, New—History.
5. Southwest, New—Social life and
customs. 6. Frontier and pioneer
life—Southwest, New. I. Title.
F786.T56 1993   93–18233
979′.02—dc20   CIP

The University Press of Florida is
the scholarly publishing agency for
the State University System of
Florida, comprised of Florida
A & M University, Florida Atlantic
University, Florida International
University, Florida State University,
University of Central Florida,
University of Florida, University of
North Florida, University of South
Florida, and University of West
Florida.

University Press of Florida
15 Northwest 15th Street
Gainesville, FL 32611

For Dottie

*who taught school in Flagstaff and put meat in
the skillet and beans in the pot while I completed
a graduate program at Arizona State College
and began a quest for Hash Knife history.*

Contents

Illustrations

Preface

A hand-forged, single-bladed hash knife, wielded by chefs, house-wives, and bunkhouse cooks, was widely used in the preparation of beef hash until two or three generations ago. A less menacing-looking kitchen tool—its more modern counterpart—is called a food chopper. Because of its flimsy double blades, the latter appears to be limited to preparing green salads.

Texas cattleman John N. Simpson chose the basic outline of the early hash knife for a cattle brand before he established a ranch in 1874 on unclaimed land two hundred miles west of Fort Worth. In the spring of 1877, he formed a partnership with rancher-banker J. R. Couts, who added capital and additional know-how to the enterprise. They registered the Hash Knife brand the following year when their ranges became a part of newly formed Parker County.

Couts sold out to Dallas banker Colonel William E. Hughes in early 1881. A year later, Simpson, Hughes, and other investors incorporated the Continental Cattle Company. The extensive land-holdings acquired by the company spread to two more ranching operations in Texas, one in Baylor County, another west of the Pecos River, and to still another in southeastern Montana.

In 1884 the Aztec Land and Cattle Company was chartered in New York City, and Hash Knife cattle from the Continental Land and Cattle Company were purchased to stock Arizona ranges of the eastern-owned company. Less than ten years after the brand was first registered, Hash Knife cattle stocked three Texas ranches, a vast Montana range, and 2 million acres in northern Arizona.

I was one of millions of American readers who became acquainted with the Hash Knife brand through a Zane Grey novel set in Arizona in 1889–90. "The Yellow Jacket Feud" was originally published in serialized form, the first installment appearing on September 21, 1929, in *Collier's Weekly*. In 1933 Harper and Brothers published it as a book, *The Hash Knife Outfit*.

Western novelist W. C. Tuttle wrote about an Arizona character he called "Hashknife" Hartley in *Hashknife of the Double Bar 8* during the same decade. The book appeared in England under the title *Arizona Ways*.

My good friend Stella Hughes wrote an award-winning book, *Hashknife Cowboy*, based on the recollections of her husband, Mack Hughes. He went to work for the famous Arizona outfit in early 1922 when he was twelve years old. His father was working for the company when the young man hired on. Mack left the Hash Knife in the mid-thirties to strike out on his own.

An old-time cowboy might ride for a number of outfits during his life, but if the Hash Knife was one of them it became his identity and his one-line biography. I was fortunate to have known several of these men. While in a graduate program at Arizona State College in Flagstaff, I wrote several papers on Canyon Diablo and Two Guns, Arizona, that included material involving Hash Knife cowboys. It was there that I learned the story of the Hash Knife included not just one ranch but five.

The writings of Zane Grey had initially inspired me and were always in the back of my mind. Another mentor of mine, the highly prolific western writer Gladwell "Toney" Richardson (who wrote under twenty-three known pen names), was thoroughly enchanted by stories on the subject. At times we sat for hours engrossed in conversations about Hash Knife cowboys.

A number of nonfiction articles about individual Hash Knife ranches have appeared over the years, but no single attempt has been made until now to tell the story of all five. Most published works have dealt with the Hash Knife cowboys themselves. Other relevant material has seemed incidental and used merely to hold stories together and provide settings for excitement and action.

Acknowledgments

I wish to offer thanks to many individuals and other sources for the use of and permissions for photographs and materials related to Hash Knife history and for their wise counsel.

I am extremely grateful for the generous help of my Arizona friend Bob Carlock, president of the Aztec Land and Cattle Company, with whom I shared photographs and history.

Also from Arizona, my longtime friend John G. Babbitt and his nephew Jim Babbitt of Flagstaff; Jo Baéza of Pinetop; Charles E. Lisitzky of Holbrook, who worked for the original A. & B. Schuster General Merchandise store from 1917 to 1966; and my friend the late Gladwell Richardson of Flagstaff.

Special thanks to my friends Mack and Stella Hughes of Eagle Creek, Arizona, for their contributions to this research. In 1984 Stella wrote an award-winning book, *Hashknife Cowboy*, based on her husband's reminiscences. The Wyrick family and the Ed Bargman photos are from the late Bill Wyrick and his daughter Dee Dee Rogers of St. Joseph, Arizona. The photograph of Barney Stiles is from his niece Mary M. Bailey of Winslow, Arizona.

Other resources in Arizona I wish to thank are Barbara Bush, Arizona Historical Society, Tucson; Janice Griffith, Old Trails Museum, Winslow; Carol Burke, Museum of Northern Arizona, Flagstaff; Bill Mulane, Cline Library, Northern Arizona University, Flagstaff; Garnette Franklin, Navajo County Historical Society,

Holbrook; Carol Patrick, Sharlot Hall Museum Library, Prescott; Elma Peterson, Flagstaff City–Coconino County Public Library, Flagstaff; Wendy Skevington, Holbrook Public Library; Laura Massey, Winslow Public Library; and Jill Cockerham of the *Winslow Mail*.

E. W. Hunt, manager of the present Hashknife Ranch in Texas, owned by his father, Ernest Hunt, was helpful in my research. Special thanks go to Dorothy Kincaid Book of Kingsland, Texas, for access to the papers of her mother, Naomi Kincaid. Thanks also to Jettie H. Russell of Seymour, Texas, and Juanita Zachry of Abilene, Texas.

Photographs and their suppliers from Texas include those of Walter Durham and Rube Neil from their grandson and grandnephew Clarence W. Durham of Mathis; Howard ("Son") Collier and the Chalk brothers from Howard Collier, Jr., of Pecos; Tom Irby, Sr., from his granddaughter Sue Kate Webb of Dallas; the Buster brothers from Charles H. Harrison of Dallas, a grandson of Charles Buster; Humphrey Hood from his daughter Betty Hood Willbanks of Bayside; and E. J. Simpson from his granddaughter Jackie Simpson McLennan of Fort Worth. Jack Jones of Seymour made copies of photographs for me, and Barney Hubbs of Pecos helped in ways too numerous to mention.

Fulton Castleberry of Ekalaka, Montana, who runs the Hash Knife brand there presently, helped in many ways. The photograph of William Lefors in Montana was furnished by Murial Jeffery of Fruitdale, South Dakota, whose stepfather, Art Lefors, was a son of William. Dave Walters of the Montana Historical Society gave valuable assistance on the Hash Knife in that state; Doug Engebretson of Belle Fouche, South Dakota, gave insight on the Axelby gang in Montana; and the Hash Knife photos from Montana were supplied by Marshall Lambert of the Carter County Museum in Ekalaka.

Thanks are due to Margaret Risley Barbour of Roswell, New Mexico, for photographs of her grandfather Burt Mossman and Hash Knife scenes. Vera Smischny of the Ellsworth County Historical Society in Kansas gave valuable help on Eugene Millett and his ranch in that state.

Jonathan Haller of the National Archives and Records Service in Washington, D.C., gave assistance with the F. A. Ames Collection of early photographs of the Aztec Land and Cattle Company in Arizona. The original cartes de visites and studio cabinet cards on the older Hash Knife operation, including many of those signed on the front by F. A. Ames, have the imprint of photographer J. C. Burge, Flagstaff, Arizona.

I also want to thank all those who gave encouragement all along the Hash Knife trails.

A reporter for the Flagstaff *Coconino Sun* described the setting for cattle operations in northern Arizona in a story of a native Texan, Walter Durham, one of the first Hash Knife cowboys in the area:

The great ranges on the plateaus of Arizona were just being discovered and occupied [in 1885] by the cattlemen of Texas, Kansas and Oklahoma, whose increasing herds were growing unwieldy, and who were rushing vast bodies of cattle over the historic trails into this region, commencing the reign of cattle owners over the vast areas, almost feudal in power, supported by small armies of riders, who were at once herdsmen and armed defenders of the real or supposed rights of the "outfits" for which they worked. They were loyal, brave and sagacious, mostly southerners, whose blood carried traces of that of cavalier ancestors, bent on adventure, quick to hate, and love and fight, who in a few years evolved into a body of western heroes who will ever be found in history, in storied romance and stirring song, as the "American Cowboy."

(February 22, 1929)

Cattlemen-Bankers
with a Vision

AFTER the Civil War, California's growing population needed beef, and pioneer Texas cowman James Robertson Couts of Parker County decided to help supply it while prices were at a premium by driving a herd of 1,000 longhorns across the Rocky Mountains.

Couts made up his herd in 1865. He hired a group of seasoned drovers, described as "cowboys of the rough and ready kind who had experience on the trail—men who knew how to handle guns and were not afraid to use them."[1] Couts himself was also skilled and predisposed to shoot if provoked. A few years earlier, in a lone, face-to-face encounter with four gunmen west of Weatherford, Texas, he killed one, wounded two, and routed the last, whose horse fell and incapacitated the fleeing rider.[2]

Because there were long distances without water if a northwesterly course was taken, the Couts herd was trailed north from Parker County through Indian Territory. Moving ten to fifteen miles a day, it entered Kansas and turned west through uninhabited land. Reaching Colorado, the drovers established a winter camp with headquarters in an abandoned mining cabin. The cattle learned to find grass underneath the snowdrifts and by spring had actually put on weight.

When the winter snows began to melt, the herd moved west to Utah. California speculators purchased the entire outfit, except for

James Robertson Couts (1833–1904). (Citizens National Bank, Weatherford, Texas)

two horses Couts held back, and hired the Couts cowboys to finish the drive for them.

The herd of cattle had cost $10 a head, and Couts sold them for around $90 each. After paying off his men, he had $50,000 left in gold currency.[3] He placed the 200 pounds of coins in small bags and wrapped them together for packing. Riding one horse and leading the other under the weight of gold, Couts headed east alone over mountains and through valleys until he reached the Platte River. He followed the waterway to the head of navigation on the Missouri and took passage by steamer to St. Louis. Here he took a packet boat down the Mississippi River to New Orleans. While waiting for a boat to Houston, Couts deposited his money in a bank, the first he had ever seen. From Houston, he returned by stagecoach to Weatherford, county seat of Parker County, where a six-month-old daughter named Margaret had been born during his absence.[4]

Impressed by the convenience and security of depositing his money for a brief time in the bank safe at New Orleans, Couts constructed a vault in the counting room of Weatherford merchant John A. Fain, and on January 1, 1870, the two men opened a banking and exchange office. They dissolved the firm six months later when Couts and Colonel William Edgar Hughes, a Weatherford attorney and former schoolmaster, opened a banking house—Hughes, Couts & Company.[5]

One of Couts & Fain's clients, Henry Warren, a government freighter in Weatherford, later became an official in Hash Knife cattle operations. He held a government contract for hauling sup-

Colonel William Edgar
Hughes (1840–1918).
(Western History De-
partment, Denver Public
Library, Denver, Colo-
rado)

plies to military forts in western Texas, and the small bank had cashed several of his drafts against the government for equipment and supplies.

Warren surrounded himself with a disorderly group of mule skinners. "At the edge of town sprawled a collection of barns, corrals, and parked wagons called 'Captain Warren's Bachelor Roost,' a place which added nothing to the dignity of the town—a rough lot of men hung out there and sometimes hard profanity could be heard— but it was tolerated by the good citizens because it was an important commercial enterprise."[6]

On May 18, 1871, a Warren wagon train carrying sacks of shelled and cracked corn to Fort Griffin was moving west over the Butterfield Overland Mail Route between Rock Creek and Salt Creek in Young County. Ten miles east of Fort Belknap it was attacked by a band of 150 Kiowas and Comanches led by Satanta (White Bear), Sitting Bear, and Big Tree. Seven of the twelve Warren teamsters, including the wagonmaster, were killed and scalped and their bodies horribly mutilated. One had his tongue cut out and was then chained to the running gear of a wagon and burned alive. Five narrowly escaped death by slipping into the cover of trees and underbrush. After sacking and burning the wagons, the Indians made off with forty-one mules.

Only the day before, from his same position of ambush, Satanta had decided against an attack on another wagon train with an army ambulance and allowed it to pass unmolested. Unknown to the chief, a passenger in this easy target was the commanding general of the U.S. Army, William Tecumseh Sherman.[7]

Speculation ran high that the Warren drafts against the government would be turned down because of the heavy loss sustained by the freighting company, but after the timely capture of those responsible for the raid and the return of the stolen mules, all claims were honored.[8]

On June 1, 1873, William E. Hughes withdrew from Hughes, Couts & Company to organize a bank in Dallas. On the same day, Couts associated himself with Henry Warren, and the name of the Weatherford banking firm was changed to J. R. Couts & Company.[9]

A fire destroyed the Parker County courthouse in Weatherford in 1874. The first brand book of the county, predating the fire, must

have been burned, because the earliest existing book for Parker
County covers the years 1874–80. It was nearly destroyed also when
it was judged to be unimportant and discarded. A thoughtful citizen
found the book in a box of trash and saved it.

Three men who were or would become prominent figures in the
history of the Hash Knife brand had registered complete or partial
monograms for cattle brands in the retrieved brand book. John
Nicholas Simpson, a native Tennesseean, had arrived on horseback
in Weatherford in 1866. He spent the winter of that first year as a
clerk in the sutler's store at the U.S. Army garrison in Fort Griffin.
When he returned to Weatherford, he opened a dry goods store.[10]
In 1872 Simpson entered the cattle business and made plans to
locate his operation 130 miles farther west on the free ranges of what
would later become Taylor County.[11] On June 8, 1874, he had

entered in the brand book what would be described in the brand lexicon as a Long S. Ten days later, Henry Warren registered a Block H Running W. On October 22 of that year, J. R. Couts entered all three of his initials within two characters, a Running JR Connected followed by a Block C.[12] These brands, along with others in the book, are believed to be reregistrations of earlier ones.

2

Choosing a Brand
and Beginning
a Cattle Empire

FOR a new ranching operation on the free ranges west of Parker County, John N. Simpson marked his cattle with a Hash Knife brand, modeled after the common kitchen tool used by cowboy cooks for chopping beef and potatoes to make hash. Originally drawn with the handle of the knife standing erect like a T with the rounded blade at the bottom end of a stout shank (fig. 1), the brand underwent early changes. Because of its resemblance to other brands like the T Anchor and Rocking T, it was later applied in an inverted position (fig. 2). Tom Irby of Weatherford, who became a foreman for the company not long after he was hired on in 1874, recalled that the ends of the crescent-shaped blade were soon extended horizontally to make the brand more difficult for rustlers to convert into other brands (fig. 3).[1] In time, the handle on the bottom of the design was also lengthened (fig. 4).

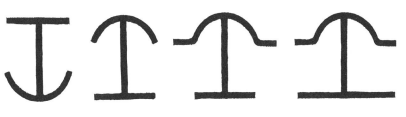

Evolution of the Hash Knife brand. (Drawing by the author)

Fig. 1.   Fig. 2.   Fig. 3.   Fig. 4.

John Nicholas Simpson (1845–1920) designed the Hash Knife brand in the early 1870s for his initial herds north and east of the Colorado River in west-central Texas. (Publicity Department, State Fair of Texas, Dallas)

Couts and Simpson recorded two brand entries for the Hash Knife in Taylor County on September 28, 1878. Proper placement was said to be on "each Side" and the road brand on the "loin and Hip." Also in the entry book was the notation "Ranche 17 miles N of Buffalo Gap."[2]

On January 23, 1879, Couts and Simpson advertised their brand and earmark in the *Fort Griffin Echo*. The cattle were identified as having a Hash Knife brand on each side in addition to a cropped

Hand-forged hash knife used by cowboy cooks to make beef hash. (Photo by the author)

right ear. The road brand for cattle was an R C on the right side and hip. Horses carried a Hash Knife brand on the left shoulder.[3]

The chosen range for the first Hash Knife herd was still buffalo country. Buffalo hunting had reached its peak in the fall of 1872, then started to decline. Some of the hunters proved to be prospective settlers who were also seeking a place to settle down. The choice buffalo ranges that would become Taylor County, Texas, in 1878 had the same potential for raising cattle.

A row of hills, the Callahan Divide, angled across the land and served as a north-south watershed. Creeks south of the hills fed the Colorado River. North of the divide, waters flowed to the Clear Fork of the Brazos River. The dividing hills offered shelter for livestock and provided building sites for stockmen.

The first cattle began arriving in the area in 1874. Simpson drove his cattle into what would be the northeast corner of the county and established the Hash Knife ranch. For the first few years, the cattle operation was run from a dugout on the brow of a hill above Cedar Creek. The other cattle that year in "the still theoretical county" were a herd of 3,700 head from Shackelford that were located in Mulberry Canyon by J. W. (Jim) Carter and Dock Grounds.[4]

Early in 1874, in the last Indian skirmish in the area, cowboys on the Jim Ned range who worked first for Sam Cholson and later for his successor, William C. Dunn, captured two members of a band of Indian raiders and hanged them.[5]

Cattle thievery, brand altering, and the unlawful slaughter of stock were major problems on the unfenced ranges. High prices for beef and the decimation of buffalo herds provoked an uncontrolled spread of cattle rustling by jobless cowboys, idle hide hunters, and

Thomas Charles Irby, Sr. (1853–1939), Hash Knife foreman from 1874 until 1889, first in Taylor County, then in Baylor County, Texas. (Courtesy of Sue Kate Webb)

marauding Indians. Individual cattlemen took drastic measures, but they needed to make a cooperative effort.

In January 1877, Simpson and James C. (Jim) Loving, son of pioneer cattleman and trailblazer Oliver Loving, published notices in several area newspapers calling for a meeting of stock growers to be held in Graham, Texas, on February 15 and 16 "to work together for the good and common interest." Another stated objective of the meeting was to organize systematic spring and fall roundups so that individual cattlemen could reclaim strays that had mixed with cattle belonging to others. Simpson called the meeting to order and nominated C. L. (Kit) Carter of San Saba County to preside over the proceedings. Simpson himself was made chairman of the resolution committee, which drafted a governing code for protection against cattle rustlers.[6] The successful two-day meeting resulted in the formation of the Stock Growers' Association of Northwest Texas, parent organization of the present Texas and Southwestern Stock Growers' Association.

On March 16, 1877, John N. Simpson and J. R. Couts of Parker County formed a partnership when the latter purchased a one-half interest in all Hash Knife cattle "running and ranging in Taylor and adjoining Counties." In addition to the brand on the left side and hip, earmarks were identified as a crop on the right ear and an over-half crop on the left ear.[7] That same year Edward James Simpson came to Texas from Tennessee and became an associate in the cattle business with his older brother John. Family members called him Jim, but newspapers usually identified him as E. J. Simpson.

The new company hauled in lumber from Weatherford and built a plank house with a long hitching rail across the front of the building. The only claim to the surrounding ranges was use and control. But by 1880, company officials felt the need to move.

Because more and more outside cattle were being turned loose on a range that had been occupied exclusively by the Hash Knife for six years, brothers John W. Buster, ranch manager, and Sterling P. Buster, company bookkeeper, headed farther west in June 1880 along the Center Line Trail to the Pecos River in search of a new range. During the ill-fated trip across arid wastelands, the men and their animals suffered severely from lack of water. At times their mules became delirious from thirst. Finally, one of the men detected

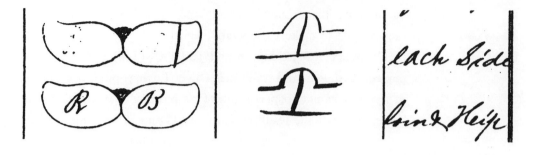

each Side

Loin & Hip

112

J.H. Simpson
To Bill of sale
Coults & Simpson

The State of Texas }
County of Taylor } Know all men by these
presents that I, J.H. Simpson
of said County and State, for and in consideration
of one dollar to me paid by Coults & Simpson of Parker
County Texas the receipt of which is hereby acknowledged Have bargained sold and range delivered and
by these presents do bargain sell and range deliver
unto said Coults and Simpson the following described
property to wit: All that stock of cattle now running
and ranging in Taylor and adjoining Counties marked
crop off the right ear over half crop the left and
Branded thus I on left side and hip
To have and to hold said stock of cattle unto them
the said Coults and Simpson their heirs and as-
signs forever Witness my hand on this the 16th day
of March A.D. 1877
                                    J.H. Simpson

State of Texas } Before me J.M. Marleton
Shackleford County } Clerk of the County Court in and
                         for said County personally appeared
J.H. Simpson who is to me well known and
acknowledged that he signed, executed and delivered
the foregoing instrument of writing for the purposes and
considerations therein specified
                Witness my Official Seal and sig-
                nature. At my Office in the Town of
                Albany this 16th day of March A.D. 1877
                J.M. Marleton Clerk C.C.S.C.
                By E.M. Canning
                        Deputy

a lone willow tree in the distance. Dangerously close to death, the two brothers were able to reach the spot and dug frantically with their hands until they found water. After a refreshing night spent beside their handmade pool, the men and their animals continued on to the Pecos without further adversity.[8]

In early 1880, the coming of the railroad to Taylor County would bisect the range of the Hash Knife cattle. The line had been chartered in 1871 by the U.S. Congress to run from Marshall, Texas, to San Diego, California, generally following the thirty-second parallel. General Granville Dodge was hired by the Texas and Pacific Railway Company as the chief engineer to build the line.

In the summer of 1876, the T & P reached Fort Worth. This became the western terminus for four years because of financial troubles. Not until 1880 did the laying of tracks resume. Two communities in Taylor County, Buffalo Gap and Phantom Hill, believed the T & P would come their way. Buffalo Gap was even designated as a supply depot for the railroad in March 1880. Land prices in both communities rose.

John N. Simpson began negotiations with the railroad company for building stock pens and locating a town 407 miles west of Marshall on what was commonly known as "Simpson's rancho."[9] He was joined by Callahan ranchers John D. Merchant and his twin brother, Clabe W. Merchant, John T. Berry of Belle Plains, and surveyor S. L. Chalk in putting together a parcel of land east of Cedar Creek, a Hash Knife pasture a mile southwest of the ranch headquarters.[10] As an inducement to bring the railroad through the site, they offered the T & P legal title to every alternate lot for half the base price of $150 an acre.[11] The other lots, owned by the investors, were to be sold to private interests or held by them individually.[12]

Opposite top: Hash Knife earmark, brand, and road brand registered in Taylor County, Texas, on September 28, 1878, by J. R. Couts and John N. Simpson. (*Record of Marks and Brands 1,* Taylor County, Texas, p. 159.) *Opposite bottom:* J. R. Couts became a partner of John N. Simpson in the Hash Knife cattle operation in Taylor County, Texas, on March 16, 1877. (*Deed Record A,* Taylor County, Texas, pp. 112–13)

In late August, the same group of ranchers met at Simpson's dugout cabin with N. C. Withers, a track locator. They reached an agreement that the railroad would go through the Hash Knife ranch in the northern part of the county, bypassing both Buffalo Gap and Phantom Hill.

Later in the year, when the tracks reached the village of Baird, twenty miles east of the Hash Knife headquarters, another meeting took place at the ranch. It was attended by a nephew of General

Couts & Simpson.
Ranch in north-east corner of Taylor Co.
P. O.. Buffalo Gap, same county.
Ranch brand same as above, on each
side: mark, crop right. Horse brand
same on left shoulder. Also road brand
R C on right side and hip.

Above: Hash Knife cowboys and chuck wagon in Taylor County, Texas, ca. 1880. (Jewell Collection, Abilene Photographic Collection, Hardin-Simmons University, Abilene, Texas.)
Right: Newspaper advertisement of the Hash Knife road brand of Couts and Simpson in Taylor County, Texas, January 23, 1879. (*Fort Griffin Echo*)

Albert Sidney Johnston of Civil War fame, J. Stoddard Johnston, who had been assigned by the railroad to locate a town site. In a signed contract, it would be located in the Hash Knife "pasture" as suggested by the group of ranchers.

Johnston decided to let the landowners select a name for the town to be built at Milepost 407. They chose the biblical name Abilene, which meant "grassy plain," but there was another reason for their choice. They hoped that it too would become a great cattle center and decided to name it for the Kansas town that had once been a successful shipping point for their Texas trail herds.[13]

The signed contract called for a 1,760-acre site on which would be built a depot, sidings, and cattle pens. The railroad and landowners would divide the profits on a sale of town lots set for March 15, 1881. Four quarter-sections of Blind Asylum Land surveyed on July 9, 1879, for Hash Knife officials J. R. Couts, John N. Simpson, E. J. Simpson, and John W. Buster became part of the original town site.[14]

In the meantime, Hash Knife cattle were being moved 200 miles west to the new range chosen earlier in the year by the Buster brothers. The *Fort Griffin Echo* reported on October 23, 1880, that "Couts & Simpson, ranching on Elm Creek [Clear Fork of the Brazos] in Taylor County, are froze out by the railroad and have moved nearly all their large stock of cattle to the Pecos river, and will continue to gather and drive as fast as possible until they are all moved."[15]

The railroad reached Abilene during the second week of January 1881. On January 26, it was announced in the press that Colonel William E. Hughes, former Weatherford resident and more recently a Dallas banker, had purchased the J. R. Couts interest in the cattle of Couts and Simpson for $77,500. In addition to the livestock Simpson owned, he was said to own one-third of the new town of Abilene, for which he had been offered $10,000.[16]

All the while, Hash Knife cattle continued to move west. In January 1881, the *Fort Griffin Echo* reported on the remaining company cattle: "Mr. John N. Simpson, of the firm of Hughes and Simpson,

John W. Buster, manager of the Hash Knife ranch in Taylor County, Texas. (Courtesy of Charles Harrison)

owners of the 'hash knife' cattle brand, spent Tuesday with friends here. He tells us that cattle on his range look better than they did one year ago. His herd is scattered but little compared with herds generally as his herders 'set 'em close' during the bad weather."[17]

The land on which the Hash Knife ranch house was located, a mile and a half northeast of the town depot, still did not belong to the company. Not until March 19, 1881, when the state granted Simpson 160 acres, did he receive a clear title to the site. The enterprising cattleman then bought the quarter-section from Couts and the adjoining quarter-sections from S. Daugherty and T. C. Green after they received their clear titles. On July 6, 1881, Simpson sold the entire 640 acres on which the Hash Knife headquarters in Taylor County was located.[18]

In addition to the immense new cattle operation west of the Pecos, the newly formed partnership of Hughes and Simpson began to expand their purchases northward to the Brazos River and beyond.

3

The Trans-Pecos Range

UGHES and Simpson registered their Hash Knife brand for cattle and horses in Pecos County on November 26, 1881, only eight months after the town lot sale in Abilene.[1] In May of that year, they had trailed Hash Knife cattle south and west through Cedar Gap to their new range, the only Texas cattle range west of the Pecos River.

Two company officials had traveled the same route the year before.[2] One trail boss, R. D. (Bob) Green, took four Hash Knife herds—10,000 head of cattle—over the 200 miles across the plains to the Horsehead Crossing of the Pecos River. The presence of Indians and the scarcity of water made the first trip difficult for his eight riders, the horse wrangler, and the cook. When the drovers reached Buzzard Roost on the Concho River, they watered and grazed the herd before starting a hazardous stretch of seventy-five miles that had no surface water. Halfway through the first lap of the drive, Indians circled the herd and made off with all the saddle horses not being ridden by drovers. The herd had to be moved the rest of the drive by cowboys on foot so the few remaining horses would be available for night work. Four days after the herd left the Concho, it reached the new camp on the Pecos.

As the second herd moved toward the Pecos on the next drive, the wind shifted from west to east, bringing the scent of water from the Concho River to the rear. It took half a day just to keep the cattle

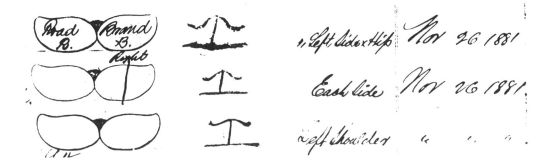

from turning back. On one of the other Green drives, when the herd strayed off course during a dense fog, the drovers chanced upon the remains of two abandoned covered wagons with the bones of oxen still yoked to each one. Nearby the skeletons of four unfortunate pioneers lay side by side.[3]

Being the first resident cattle in the area, the Hash Knife herds roamed at will wherever grass and water were found, over a 100-mile pasture up and down the Pecos from Grand Falls to the New Mexico line. To the southwest, the range was limitless.[4] Otto Tinnian, an area cattleman born in the pioneer community of Toyah in 1883, recalled the company's domination of the range: "The Hash Knife Outfit claimed that their range was from west of the Pecos River to the Rio Grande to El Paso; thence to a point on the Guadalupe, and then down the Delaware."[5]

No Texas cattle range lay west of the Pecos except that used by 20,000 Hash Knife cattle. It was described in mid-October 1881 as "big enough to feed all the cattle and sheep in Texas."[6] The country was well suited for raising stock, from the river through the Toyah Basin and into the foothills of the Guadalupe Mountains. Even the mountains and their spur ridges that extended southward were covered with grama grass. The hillsides were sprinkled with buckeye, wild cherry, oak, cedar, pine, cottonwood, and walnut trees, and the Hash Knife ranges of the trans-Pecos included antelope, black-tailed deer, and cinnamon bear. One contemporary account added that even Mexican lions could be found "without looking for them."[7]

The company maintained cattle camps along streams or at spring sites. Two men were stationed at each line camp on the outside limits of the range to ride the perimeter and turn back strays. These

Horsehead Crossing of the Pecos River. (Courtesy of Barney Hubbs)

riders spent the winters in what they called a "chosy," a simple dugout with a chimney and a door in the side of a bank.[8]

The first year that Howard T. (Son) Collier worked for the Hash Knife, the company branded 9,999 calves. He said they would have found one more had they known their total count. A branding team did nothing but mark cattle, starting about thirty miles below Pecos City and working its way north from one roundup to another all the way to the New Mexico line.[9]

Collier described the spring gathering of cattle on the open range: "The Hash Knife people had two trail outfits for the first round-up in the spring. Each outfit consisted of 11 men with 66 horses and, of course, a chuck wagon. There were eight herd riders, the cook, the 'hoss' wrangler and the trail boss. It was the job of the horse wrangler to move the horses from camp to camp and take care of them. Each cowboy was allowed six horses, ridden by no one but himself. They worked the horses hard and there had to be frequent changes. It was said that the cowboy got up before he could see and went to bed when he couldn't see."[10]

Howard T. (Son) Collier (*center*) flanked by the Chalk brothers of Toyah, Texas. All three were employed as horse wranglers and bronc riders by the Hash Knife outfit west of the Pecos River in the 1880s. (Courtesy of Howard T. Collier, Jr.)

The company maintained a horse ranch near Screwbean Springs in the Rustler Hills ten miles west of Orla. A gang of rustlers who preyed on cattlemen at the time as far east as Buffalo Gap near Abilene made their headquarters southwest of the Hash Knife horse ranch. They were ultimately trailed and captured by cowboys who hanged all five from a cottonwood tree at what came to be known as Rustler Springs.[11] Large-scale cattle rustling flourished in the area in the late 1800s, according to John D. Alexander, "The Screwbean Kid," who began cowboy life there in the spring of 1909.[12]

Some of the Hash Knife cattle—an average of 5,000 steer yearlings—were driven each spring from the Pecos River to a feeder ranch maintained by the company in Montana, where they were fattened for the northern markets.[13] The long drive took six or seven months.[14]

Mississippi-born A. Travis (Trav) Windham had moved to the Pecos River area in 1879 and soon hired on with the Hash Knife. His wife, the former Annie Goedeke of Abilene, Texas, and their six-month-old daughter made the trip to the Pecos range on the Texas and Pacific in 1881. They got off the train at Toyah and rode a freight wagon to the ranch house forty miles north at a frontier headquarters on the west side of the river that later became the community of Arno. They would not see another woman for eighteen months.[15]

Windham became the range boss for the Hash Knife. He would work for the outfit for five years before moving to the Seven Rivers Cattle Company on the east side of the Pecos River, the first outfit to have cattle interests in that area.

Windham and other cowboys representing the Hash Knife, the Mill Iron, the W, the 101, and other ranches on both sides of the river, are credited with conducting the first organized rodeo in the United States.[16] The Pecos City contest grew out of a discussion among cowboys gathered at Bill Camp's saloon. They decided to hold a "roping match" to determine the best among the outfits. It took place on July 4, 1883, in an open field adjoining the county courthouse with 500 nonpaying spectators. Two men held the yearling steer that was to be roped and tied, releasing it on signal. The contestant had to chase and rope the steer from his horse, dismount, and tie its legs together to complete the timed event. Hash Knife cowboy Trav Windham, the winner with a time of twenty-two seconds, received a $25 prize.[17]

In March 1885, citizens and taxpayers in the Pecos Valley, a part of western and southwestern Tom Green County, petitioned the Texas legislature to create other counties from areas attached to Midland and Reeves counties for judicial and land-surveying purposes. Their major complaint was that the county seat at San Angelo was 250 or 350 miles away, and residents doing official business had to travel through six counties, not including Midland County, to reach their own county offices. Signers of the petition included the notorious gunfighter Clay Allison and his brother-in-law J. S. McCulloch. Trav Windham, former Hash Knife cowboy, signed as manager of the Seven Rivers Cattle Company.[18]

Trav Windham, Hash Knife cowboy of Pecos, Texas, and one of the organizers of the first rodeo in America. (Courtesy of Barney Hubbs)

Tintype of Charles W. Buster, manager, and Sterling P. Buster, company bookkeeper, of the Hash Knife ranch west of the Pecos River in Texas. The copy of the tintype has been reversed to obtain the correct image. (Courtesy of Charles Harrison)

On April 30, 1885, the second chattel mortgage on record in newly created Reeves County, Texas, was filed in the amount of $358,000 with Henry Warren as mortgagor, representing the Aztec Land and Cattle Company in Arizona, and E. J. Simpson, trustee of the Continental Land and Cattle Company, established by Hughes and John Simpson in 1882. The property mortgaged was all the Hash Knife cattle "Ranched and located in Reeves C. Texas." Payment dates were set for September 1, 1885, June 15, 1886, and June 15, 1887.[19]

Following the sale of the cattle, the Continental Land and Cattle Company purchased the W Ranch, which lay on the east side of the Pecos. Charles W. Buster, who turned over the Hash Knife cattle to the Arizona buyers, took charge of the W.[20] The transaction involved 14,000 head of cattle and 365 horses and mules. The new ranch operation was placed on the 1886 tax rolls in far-off San Angelo, where the company was required to record legal transactions. Real property value totaled $118,675, including stock, ranch equipment, and miscellaneous property.[21]

The ranch of Clay Allison, one of the most deadly gunmen in the Old West, bordered the W Ranch on the north near Pope's Crossing, forty-five miles north of Pecos City. On December 15, 1886, Allison purchased a town lot and moved his family into Pecos City so that his older daughter would have access to good schools and a piano teacher. On July 3, 1887, while driving alone back to his ranch in a heavily loaded wagon, he fell or was thrown from the vehicle in Screwbean Draw north of Pecos City and was crushed to death under the wheels.[22]

The Continental Land and Cattle Company registered the W brand in Reeves County on March 11, 1899.[23] Although the mark had the look of a Running W, some cowboys called it the Walking W.

4

Between the Forks
of the Brazos

HUGHES and Simpson's official registration of the Hash Knife brand in Baylor County is dated January 23, 1882. It shows the placement of the cattle brand on each side, the horse brand on the left shoulder, and the road brand for both cattle and horses on the left side.[1]

At the same time Hash Knife cattle were being trailed west to the Pecos River, Hughes and Simpson were adding to their already extensive holdings. Early in 1881, they acquired grazing rights to thousands of acres of upper Brazos River range, north of Taylor County, which had been surveyed with a lariat from horseback.[2] During the next season, they also received 25,000 head of cattle at $12 per head, not including or counting calves, and 1,000 horses from E. B. Millett & Bros. in what was called the largest livestock transaction ever carried out in northwest Texas.[3] The broad, free-hand Snake M brand of Eugene, Alonzo, and Hiram Millett, which looked something like a twisting serpent, was replaced by the Hash Knife of the new owners.[4]

In 1881, Hughes and Simpson also made large investments in land and cattle northward between the Pease River and the Red River, including the Bridle Bit, the DV, the Diamond D, and the Mill Iron. A dugout headquarters was established in Hall County, Texas. Following the purchase of the Mill Iron spread on Bitter

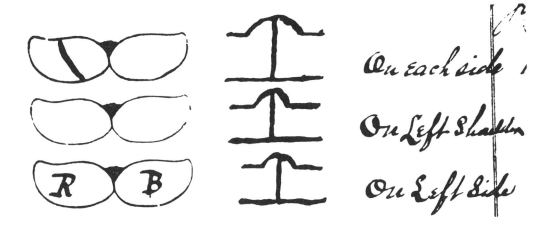

On Each side

On Left Shoulder

On Left Side

Lake, near the Pease River, the Mill Iron became a widespread company brand.[5]

On April 28, 1882, the Continental Cattle Company was incorporated in St. Louis, Missouri, primarily for the "buying, branding, selling, and grazing of Live Stock." W. E. Hughes, John N. Simpson, E. C. Sterling, W. L. Huse, and James W. Bell were named as trustees in the new corporation, whose capital stock was placed at $1 million and divided into 10,000 shares at $100 each.[6]

Hughes and Simpson bought two 640-acre parcels of land on June 20, 1882, from Eugene B. and Alonzo Millett. One tract was on the Brazos River; the other was vaguely defined as being in "Baylor (formerly (Cook[e]) County," Texas. On the same day, another, larger tract of land changed hands, involving the same buyers and sellers. It was described as "One Third of a League of Land in Baylor County State of Texas on the waters of Millers Creek."[7] (It would have been 1,490 acres based on the old standard of measurement used for former Mexican lands.)

Captain Eugene B. Millett, senior member of the Millett brothers cattle business, along with Texas cattleman William C. Irvin, had established the Miller Creek spread on the upper Brazos River in 1874.[8] During that year, with longtime business associate Major Seth Mabry, Millett also began buying large numbers of cattle for the 1875 drive to northern markets. Mabry went to New York and secured the government contract to supply beef on the hoof for the Sioux reservations at $12 a head for cows and $20 for steers. Millett

Captain Eugene Bartlett Millett (1838–1916), who sold his extensive Brazos River ranges to the Hash Knife in 1881. (Ellsworth County Historical Society, Ellsworth, Texas)

was quoted as saying that they proposed "to buy up the entire 1875 drive of cattle, Indian contracts and all."[9]

By spring, Millett and Mabry owned, by drive and contract, 52,000 cattle, mostly three-year-olds and up. As if this proposed cattle movement were not ambitious enough, the two united their interests with those of Texas cattlemen John O. Dewees and James F. Ellison, who owned or controlled another 50,000 head. For sheer numbers, the combined undertaking is one of the greatest cattle drives out of Texas in the annals of trail driving. The cattle, destined for a distribution point at Ogallala, Nebraska, were received at a camp established near San Antonio. At one time, herds were strung out from there to southern Kansas. Millett and Mabry bought 900 horses for the drive and employed 275 men.[10] Before the mammoth drive, Captain Millett picked out 3,000 cows with calves and turned them over to his brother, Hiram (Hi) Millett, to help stock their Baylor County ranch.[11]

The Millett ranch bought by Hughes and Simpson included parts of what are now Baylor, Throckmorton, Knox, and Wilbarger counties. A. P. (Ott) Black worked first for the Milletts and then for the new owners. He described the seasonal ranges used by both companies during their back-to-back cattle operations in the Brazos country: "The summer range stretched about forty miles from the Wichita breaks south to Elm Creek [Clear Fork of the Brazos]. The winter range ran from the Wichita breaks on the south to Beaver Creek in Eilbarger [sic] County on the north. It was about sixty-five miles across both ranges. They had eight line camps, sixteen line riders and one line boss."[12]

"The line of circumference around the range of the main herd was fully sixty miles," recalled Millett, who laid out the ranch. "Along this extended line fully equipped camps were established every six or eight miles. The herders were placed at each camp, riding each way until meeting a rider from an adjoining station. In this way a close tab was kept on everything on the range."[13]

In order to combat Indian, half-breed Mexican, renegade, and outlaw cattle raiders, the Milletts operated the range under an organization and system equal to that of a well-commanded army camp. The buildings, constructed of native stone, were arranged like a fortress and surrounded by a stone wall five feet high with only one gate. A combination warehouse-blockhouse, well supplied for long sieges, was built to serve as a fort against attacks by Indians or cattle raiders. It had gun ports every four feet on the north side and a good view in all directions. Portions of the great cattle trails leading to Dodge City, Hunnewell, and Montana passed within sight of the headquarters.

The Millett brothers and their cowboys were a rough group of men, and the ranch was called "one of the toughest spots this side of Hell."[14]

John Simpson, the working member of the Hughes and Simpson partnership, learned how the place earned its reputation when he rode up to the ranch on horseback from Dallas, leading a pack mule carrying gold to pay for the cattle. He arrived just in time to see a gun battle between four horse thieves and four members of a Shackelford County sheriff's posse, including the man who came along to reclaim his property. From behind the rock fence in front of the

Ruins of the fortress-like grub room of the Millett ranch partly destroyed by a flood in the 1880s. (Baylor County Free Library, Seymour, Texas)

ranch house, the offenders opened fire at the lawmen as they approached. Three lawmen went down with bullet wounds, and the owner of the stolen horses reined about and escaped on his horse. Deputy Henry Herron credited Simpson with saving his life by intervening when the outlaw leader walked up to kill the lawman, who lay helpless on the ground.[15]

Following the sale of his Baylor County ranch, Captain Millett moved to eastern Kansas for a few years before settling down in 1886 on Idavale, his ranch, named for his wife, Ida, on Smoky River near the mouth of Bluff Creek in Ellsworth County.

With the change in ownership of the Baylor County ranch, the Continental Cattle Company inherited a few hard characters as well as an infamous reputation. Millett foreman Tom Peeler, son-in-law of part owner William C. Irvin, was described as a "traveling arsenal," with specially made cartridge loops on his chaps down to the knees, two six-shooters, and a Winchester rifle or breech-loading shotgun in the saddle. Only a year before the sale, Millett cowboys had run some local officials out of Seymour, the county seat, prompting the governor to send in Texas Rangers to protect the sovereignty of the county. In the Millett sale, the Hash Knife also received its own Boot Hill, already stocked with unfortunate cowboys killed in accidents or gunfights.[16]

Tom Irby was selected the official counter in the transfer of cattle

Cowboys with Hash Knife and Mill Iron cattle and horses depicted in a stock certificate of the Continental Land and Cattle Company that was issued to Jno. N. Simpson on February 18, 1884. (Hughes Collection, Santa Fe, New Mexico)

from the Milletts; he later became ranch foreman for Hughes and Simpson in Baylor County after he helped locate 10,000 head of company cattle in the Pecos country. During the count, Millett cowboys were found to be adding to the tally by running some cattle around and around a small hill on which Irby was perched. The final total in a recount was around 25,000.[17]

The Mill Iron Cattle Company and the Continental Cattle Company were reorganized at the company offices in Dallas on January 21, 1884, as the Continental Land and Cattle Company. Section 1 of the charter reads, "Said Company is formed for the purpose of purchasing lands, and for holding selling and conveying the same in lots or otherwise, and for the raising, ranching and breeding of live stock such as Horses, Cattle, Sheep and Goats, and for the improvement of the breed of domestic animals, and for the Sale of the same in the State of Texas, as well as in the States of Colorado, Kansas, Nebraska, Missouri & Illinois, and in the Territories of Wyoming, Montana, Dakota, Arizona, New Mexico and the Indian Territories, and Old Mexico, and in such other places as the prosecution of the business of the Company may require."[18] Directors or trustees of the new corporation were W. E. Hughes, John N. Simpson, and Henry Warren, who all resided in Texas, and E. C. Sterling, James W. Bell, W. L. Huse, and John Whittaker, who all lived in St. Louis,

Missouri. Hughes was named president and Simpson manager of the expanding corporation that now had cattle on three Texas ranches, as well as 25,000 to 70,000 head in the Wyoming, Montana, and Dakota territories.[19]

In December 1885, Henry Warren resigned as a director, and he was replaced by John W. Buster. In 1888, Simpson succeeded Hughes as president, but he soon began taking a less active part in the corporation, concentrating more on his banking interests in Dallas and on his landholdings elsewhere. Buster became general manager of the corporation. The company cattle industry in Texas itself was becoming more centered in the Mill Iron to the northwest, where Hughes eventually became the sole owner.[20]

The Millett base of operations on Miller Creek was partly abandoned by the Hash Knife when the company built another headquarters on a hill overlooking the Brazos River in Baylor County. The date 1885 was chiseled into a large oblong stone on the outside of the building.[21] A new headquarters for the Mill Iron was also established in 1888, three miles south of Estelline at an old ranch site

Abandoned headquarters of the Hash Knife ranch built in Baylor County, Texas, in 1885. (Baylor County Free Library, Seymour, Texas)

known as 62 Wells. The land had originally been claimed in 1862 and had numerous springs that were later converted into wells.[22] The old Millett spread in Baylor County was discontinued as a Hash Knife range in 1889. In September of that year, the Mill Iron purchased an additional 46,000 acres in Hall, Motley, Childress, and Cottle counties, giving the expanding operation control of an aggregate range of 162,000 acres.[23]

Tom Irby, company foreman in Baylor County, lived in the old Millett stone headquarters with its rock corrals and outbuildings from 1881 to 1889. When the Hash Knife vacated, he moved into Seymour and became a businessman and an active participant in community affairs.[24]

Edward C. Sterling of St. Louis, an officer and stockholder in the Continental Land and Cattle Company, bought the 6,492 6/10-acre Hash Knife holdings of the company in Baylor County for $25,000 on May 12, 1899, ending nearly twenty years of the Hash Knife presence. The grazing lands consisted of eleven different surveys. Included in the transaction were all houses, farm machinery, wagons, fencing, and so on. According to the terms of the sale as set forth in the deed, "The intention is to hereby sell and convey all the lands, rights and equities owned by the Continental Land & Cattle Company in the County of Baylor State of Texas."[25]

Less than a hundred yards west of the headquarters of what was once "one of the toughest spots this side of hell," Sterling built a large house for a dance hall and a gambling casino to entertain his friends. Later converted into a family residence, it was sold in 1906.[26]

5

A New Range 1,200 Miles North

THE Hash Knife brand was recorded in Montana on October 4, 1882, with the placement designated for cattle on the right ribs and hip and the brand for horses on the right side. A crop on the right ear was also registered for cattle.[1] Word soon spread, however, that if an animal had a Hash Knife brand, no matter where it was, it belonged to the Continental Cattle Company. A defiant notice that the Texans would put the mark anywhere they wanted to appeared in 1885 in the first brand book of the Montana Stock Growers' Association. In locating the brand placement, the company lay claim to any animal with the Hash Knife on the side and hip of either side, on both sides, or "on any part of the animal."[2]

The HS (Hughes and Simpson) brand was recorded on October 2, 1882, two days before the Hash Knife was registered. Its placement was assigned to the right ribs and hip for cattle and on the right thigh for horses. At that time the company address for Hughes and Simpson on the northern range was Camp Crook, Dakota Territory.[3]

In 1879, John Simpson had selected a distant northern range for Hash Knife cattle on the Little Missouri River, Box Elder Creek, Little Beaver Creek, and a small part of the Powder River drainage in the territories of Montana and Dakota. He later built cow camps to receive trail herds from Texas.[4] The company started a ranch on the Little Missouri, twenty miles downstream from a site with a

JOHN N. SIMPSON, Manager,
Dallas, Tex.

WILLIAM LEFORS, Foreman,
Stoneville, Mont.

W. E. HUGHES, President,
Dallas, Texas.

E. C. STERLING, Vice President,
St. Louis, Mo.

JAS. W. BELL, Secretary and Treasurer, St. Louis, Mo.

CONTINENTAL LAND & CATTLE CO.

Capital, $3,000,000.

P. O. Ad., St. Louis, Mo.

Range, Little Missouri River, and Box Elder and Little Beaver Creeks, in Montana and Dakota.

Horse Vent, thus ——— on thigh.

Cattle branded on both sides.

Other brands on Cattle,

HS on right side and hip.

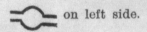 on right side. ⊃⊂ on left side.

Other brands on Horses,

HS on right shoulder and thigh.

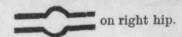 on right hip.

Other brands on both Horses and Cattle,

⊥ { on side and hip.
{ on both sides.
{ on any part of animal.

W { on both sides.
{ on either side.

saloon and seven or eight log shacks called Stoneville. This early ranch was only a cow camp at the mouth of Horse Creek, built for the purpose of holding the range. The name Stoneville was changed to Alzada in 1890.

Hash Knife herds were some of the first southern cattle to locate north of the Black Hills. The immigrant longhorns from Texas were called "pilgrim cattle," and area newspapers prophetically warned they would not survive the cruel winters.[5]

In April 1882, a herd of cattle belonging to the old Continental Cattle Company was assembled in Texas and pointed north. They arrived on Box Elder Creek on July 17. One of the trail bosses stood on Bell Tower Butte overlooking the lush grasslands and his Texas longhorns and proclaimed, "This is it, turn them loose."[6]

The home ranch for Hash Knife cattle on northern pastures was established by range manager William Lefors on Box Elder Creek, twenty miles east of the present Ekalaka, Montana. A hay meadow and horse camp for HS horses were located on the Box Elder southeast of the Chalk Buttes near the mouth of Prairie Dog Creek. Another ranch for horses was established about eight miles northeast of Ekalaka in what became known as the Hash Knife Basin or, perhaps more properly, the HS Basin.

Like other cattle companies, the Hash Knife occupied the land without benefit of legal transaction. Under the existing free-range policy, cattlemen found a location, erected a headquarters, and claimed the surrounding range. If a company chose to sell out, it merely transferred its rights to the range. These rights were normally respected by others, but sometimes a company had to be tough enough to protect its range by force. Hash Knife cowboys were so capable of doing so that outsiders called them "a rawhide outfit."[7]

George Axelby helped drive one of the first Hash Knife herds from the Pecos range in Texas to Montana but soon quit the company and became a buffalo hunter. In 1882 or 1883, Indians raided his camp and destroyed his accumulation of hides for the season. To get even, Axelby began stealing Indian ponies with such wild abandon that his vengeance attracted national attention. One *New York Sun* correspondent wrote: "An Indian is Mr. Axelby's detestation. He kills them at sight if he can. He considers that Indians have no right to own ponies and he takes their ponies whenever he can."[8]

According to John W. Buster, a Hash Knife executive in Montana, Axelby rode into their cow camp in 1883 with eighty Indian ponies and a young cowboy he called "the Kid." While the two were having a noon meal, Indians rode into sight. The Kid quickly drove the stolen horses up the river; Axelby moved out of camp alone and

William Lefors, Hash Knife foreman in Montana. (Courtesy of Muriel Jeffery)

stationed himself in a nearby gully. When the Indians got within a hundred yards, Axelby opened up with a steady stream of gunfire, killing or wounding several Indians. The others turned their horses and fled.[9]

Even the great Sioux warrior Young-Man-Afraid-of-His-Horses did not escape the wrath of George Axelby and the gang that surrounded him. In the winter of 1883, the influential Indian leader lost all of his horses to the thieves and was forced to give up his hunt for buffalo on the Grand River in Dakota Territory. He reported his loss at the Pine Ridge Agency, and federal lawmen were dispatched with instructions to "exterminate" the gang.[10] Other state and local law agencies joined in the action.

In addition to Axelby, two or three other members of the gang were said to be former Hash Knife employees. A Deadwood (Dakota Territory) newspaper, the *Black Hill Times,* noted that they were all members of "the cowboy specie" that had originated in

Texas and spread throughout the northern cattle country: "They have ridden through the streets, whooping and yelling like savages, and shooting their pistols at signs or anything that came in their way. They have made day and night hideous, and they make strangers think that there was neither law, order or decency in the country."[11]

Jesse B. Pruden, a member of the gang, was arrested in Miles City, Montana, on February 3, 1884, and preparations were made to escort him to Lou Stone's ranch (Stoneville) on the Little Missouri River. He was to be picked up there by the officers from Dakota. George Axelby heard of the capture and resolved to rescue Pruden while he was being transferred.

With neither Dakota group knowing the location of the other, a posse from Deadwood and one from Spearfish spent the night of February 13 at road ranches only two miles apart. Upon their arrival in Stoneville, the Spearfish posse learned that the Axelby gang had spent the night at the saloon owned by Stone only two hundred yards from his home and was still there. When the six outlaws emerged from the saloon shortly after dawn, the Spearfish posse opened fire. The Deadwood lawmen were close enough to hear the shots and rushed to the scene.[12]

Below left: George Axelby. (*Belle Fouche* [South Dakota] *Bee,* September 4, 1941.) *Below right:* Humphrey Hood (1861–1917), brother-in-law of E. J. Simpson and a Hash Knife official in Montana. (Courtesy of Betty Hood Willbanks)

The "Stoneville Battle" of February 14, 1884, resulted in the eventual deaths of five men. Two were killed on the spot, one was tracked down and killed the following day, another was taken out of the Spearfish hospital twelve days after the gunfight and hanged by a band of masked men, and the fifth died of his wounds six months later. The fatalities were Deputy Sheriff Jack O'Hara from Spearfish, two innocent cowboy bystanders, and two gang members. Although suffering from a thigh wound, George Axelby escaped. It was reported that he and the Kid were both seen later in South America.

Despite a severe head wound, outlaw Hank Campbell, also called Jack, John, William, or Bill Campbell in written accounts, made it into the bushes, crawled five miles down the ice-covered Little Missouri, and obtained shelter at another ranch house. There he wrote a message to Humphrey Hood, a Hash Knife official and a future brother-in-law of company executive E. J. Simpson: "Dear Hood: I was badly wounded in the head during the fight yesterday and my horse killed. The boys were all shot to pieces and scattered. For God's sake send me a horse by bearer as soon as it is dark enough to get away from the officers."[13]

One of the lawmen intercepted the note and instructed the bearer to comply with the request. The delivery of the horse was delayed until nightfall so the officer and a posse could follow the man and horse to the cabin where the outlaw was hidden. The horse was tied to the corral, and the messenger went to the door and told Campbell the horse was there. When Campbell emerged from the cabin he was ordered to throw up his hands, but the desperate outlaw began firing in the direction of the posse. Fifteen bullets in the return fire slammed into his body, killing him instantly.[14]

Still standing in "Boot Row" in the Alzada graveyard as late as 1939 were five bullet-ridden headboards, reminders of the violent deaths of one lawman, two cowboys, and two horse thieves, all victims of the gunfight at old Stoneville in 1884.[15]

At first, Hash Knife cattle were trailed north over the southern portion of the established Fort Griffin and Dodge City Trail, frequently called the Western Trail. In 1885, however, the southern part of the trail was moved west to avoid Indian harassment.

The new trail led northwest from Seymour, Texas, crossing the

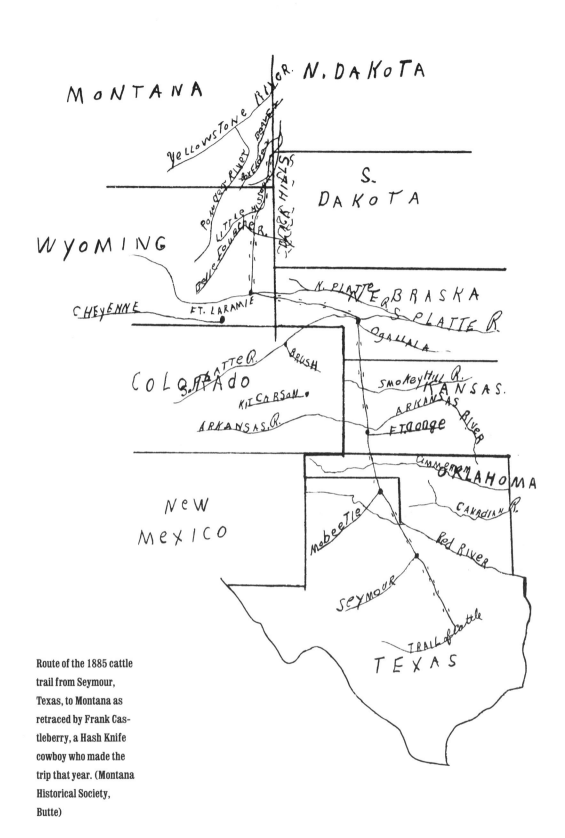

MONTANA

N. DAKOTA

Yellowstone River

Powder River

BEAVER

Boxelder

LITTLE MISSOURI

Belle Fourche R.

S. DAKOTA

BLACK HILLS

WYOMING

CHEYENNE

FT. LARAMIE

N. PLATTE RIVER

NEBRASKA

S. PLATTE R.

Ogallala

COLORADO

S. PLATTE R.

BRUSH

KIT CARSON

ARKANSAS R.

SMOKEY HILL R.

KANSAS

ARKANSAS RIVER

FT. DODGE

CIMMERON R.

OKLAHOMA

CANADIAN R.

NEW MEXICO

Mobeetie

Red River

Seymour

TRAIL of cattle

TEXAS

Route of the 1885 cattle trail from Seymour, Texas, to Montana as retraced by Frank Castleberry, a Hash Knife cowboy who made the trip that year. (Montana Historical Society, Butte)

Wichita, Pease, and Red rivers to Mobeetie, the first town built in the Texas Panhandle. From there it crossed the Canadian and the Cimarron and went up the "Government freight trail" to Dodge Crossing in Kansas on the Arkansas River. The cattle continued north, fording the South Platte at Ogallala, Nebraska, and then to the North Platte. Here the trail turned west and followed the river upstream for ninety miles. It struck the Government Road at Fort Laramie, then went north to Fort Robinson. Bypassing the Black Hills on the west to Stoneville (Alzada), Montana, it proceeded down the Little Missouri to the mouth of Box Elder Creek.[16] A drive to Montana, averaging 2,500 cattle, was on the trail about three months.

The trail had to be moved west again the following year because of a Kansas quarantine against the entry of Texas cattle that might be tick-infested. Northbound herds in 1886 were driven over a new route across the Neutral Strip, entering Colorado in the southeast corner and continuing north just inside the eastern boundary to a brief stopover for drovers at Trail City on the Arkansas River. The town, built to entertain trail-weary cowboys and take their money, was less than a year old, but it was already becoming known as "that hell-hole on the Arkansas."[17] The trail then veered slightly north-east before turning directly north to Ogallala and beyond.

On April 27, 1886, the Montana-based Hash Knife outfit recorded their other Texas cattle brands, the Mill Iron and the Bridle Bit.[18]

On June 9 and 10, 1886, the first three herds on the new trail reached Trail City; two of them belonged to the Continental Land and Cattle Company. All three trail bosses were promptly arrested for entering Colorado without health clearances for their herds and for not confining the herds to the trail agreed upon and were placed under $1,000 bond. When it was determined that the drovers had not wantonly disregarded the laws, they were allowed to proceed north with their herds.[19]

Records for the spring of 1886 kept by C. H. Marselus, a cattle inspector stationed at Trail City, suggest the vast number of long-horn cattle trailed north from Texas during the 1880s by cowboys of the Continental Land and Cattle Company. Seven company herds, numbering 18,445 head of cattle, passed through in June and a single herd of 2,850 head in July. Out of the total number of 21,295

Hash Knife and Mill Iron
cattle corralled at the
Standing Rock Indian
Agency, Dakota Terri-
tory, on beef issue day in
the late 1880s. (Mon-
tana Historical Society,
Butte)

cattle, 14,875 carried the Hash Knife brand, and the remaining 6,400 the Mill Iron brand.[20] The section of the trail in eastern Wyoming, from the Cheyenne River north to the Little Missouri, soon became known to drovers as "the Hashknife Trail."[21]

A number of Indian reservations in Montana, Wyoming, and Dakota were handy markets for the Hash Knife and Mill Iron cattle. There Northern Plains Indians were issued regular beef allotments by the federal government to prevent starvation. Assistant range manager Jack Talbert delivered 2,500 steers to the Standing Rock Agency at Fort Yates in 1883, and a government contract specified that the company was to deliver 350 head to the post from time to time as needed. Ott Black said the "maiden name" of Talbert was Jack Taylor and that he was believed to have been connected with the Jesse James bunch in some way.[22]

The major northern market for the Continental Land and Cattle Company was Chicago. Cattle were trailed to Mingusville, now Wibaux, or to Fallon and loaded on railway cars for shipment. It was estimated that the company shipped fifty-four carloads of beef cattle from Dickinson, Dakota, to Chicago during the week of August 15, 1886.[23]

Some of the Continental Land and Cattle Company cowboys in Montana were disorderly and mean, throwing the reputation of others into question. The term *Hash Knife boys* sounded dangerous to those outside the company and more often than not suggested trouble or alarm. John O. Bye, whose father began ranching on the Little Missouri in 1886, wrote about the diverse backgrounds of Hash Knife hands: "Some . . . were picked up on the trail coming up and some . . . joined the 'wagons' after the outfits arrived in the north, 'locals,' as they were called. Many of them worked for other outfits before they joined the Hash Knife. Some left enough history so that a thumb nail sketch can be given of their life and activities. Of some you had better not inquire their names and former range."[24]

Bye then reprinted part of a regional poem that he felt appropriately described Hash Knife cowboys. It mentions a saloon in the cow town of Little Missouri opposite the present North Dakota town of Medora:

Some came for lungs and some for jobs,
And some for booze at Big-mouth Bob's,
Some to punch cattle, some to shoot,
Some for a vision, some for loot;
Some for views and some for vice,
Some for faro, some for dice;
Some for the joy of a galloping hoof,
Some for the prairie's spacious roof,
Some to forget a face, a fan,
Some to plumb the heart of man;
Some to preach and some to blow,
Some to grab and some to grow,
Some in anger, some in pride,
Some to taste, before they died,
Life served hot and a la cartee—
And some to dodge a necktie-party.[25]

Ott Black quit "the Hashknives" in March 1886, after the company ruled that no cowboy in its employ could have cattle of his own. All of those who did have cattle when the rule went into effect were told they must either trade them for shares in the company or keep the cattle and quit. Seven Hash Knife riders were affected by the ruling.[26]

Another cowboy who left the company, Billy Powers, drifted down into the Indian Territory, fell in with the Dalton brothers, and was killed with three other members of the outlaw gang on October 5, 1892, during an unsuccessful attempt to rob two banks at the same time in Coffeyville, Kansas.[27]

Four other Hash Knife boys who worked with Ott Black left Montana and hired on with the Aztec Land and Cattle Company in Arizona. R. M. (Bob) Gillespie got involved there in the Pleasant Valley War, was shot off his horse, and crawled eight miles before he got help. He later went to New Mexico. Oscar McLean got drunk one night in Winslow and shot at the swinging lantern of a railroad conductor, missed, and hit the man in the leg. He was forced to become a drifter. Broncho Jim held up a dance hall in Winslow and received a shotgun load in the face. Walter Durham, the other Hash Knife cowboy who left Montana, worked for the Hash Knife outfit in Arizona before becoming a respected cattleman in Flagstaff.[28]

Hash Knife roundup with the "morning circlers" on the Little Missouri River in Montana, May 27, 1890. (E. W. "Pecos River Dick" Turbiville Collection, Carter County Museum, Ekalaka, Montana)

Jeff Lefors, brother of William Lefors, Hash Knife range manager in Montana, also made his way to Arizona and hired on with the Aztec Land and Cattle Company.

Difficult days lay ahead for the Continental Land and Cattle Company in Montana. On the northern ranges during the terrible winter of 1886 and spring of 1887, it sustained losses estimated at 90 percent.[29] Another source claimed that all but 600 of the 30,000 Hash Knife steers trailed from Texas perished in what came to be known as the "big die up."[30]

In June 1887, two Hash Knife trail herds, 3,000 head of cattle each, were en route from Texas to Montana. At the same time, co-owner John Simpson was foretelling the ultimate fate of open ranges and long trail drives in an interview in Denver. "The day of the great cattle ranges is about over," he said. "There will be smaller herds which will have to be fed in the winter. Montana is a good country but has been overstocked."[31]

Meanwhile, back at the ranch in West Texas, the Continental Land and Cattle Company was involved in a large-scale delivery of Hash Knife cattle from the Pecos River to a new company in Arizona. The sale resulted from a combination of a prolonged drought in Texas, Eastern financing, government land grants, and the extension of a transcontinental railroad through northern Arizona.

6

The Hash Knife Outfit in the Arizona Territory

HE Hash Knife was registered as the stock brand for both cattle and horses by Captain Henry Warren in Apache County, Arizona, on June 2, 1885.[1] The first newspaper advertisement giving public notice of the new Arizona brand appeared in the *St. Johns Herald*, published in the courthouse town of Apache County on June 11, 1885. The cattle range was defined as Apache and Yavapai counties.[2] Warren registered the Hash Knife in Yavapai County on August 22, 1885, with this notation: "Brand placed on Cattle, on both Sides of Animal, and on horses, brand is placed on left Shoulder of Animal—Ear Mark for Cattle is 'Grub' the right."[3] A grub mark, the cruelest of all earmarks, normally meant the severance of an entire ear.[4] A registered drawing of the Hash Knife mark, however, reveals no more than an exaggerated ear crop.

As a result of the congressional Land Grant Act of 1866, the Atlantic and Pacific Railroad Company was authorized to complete a segment of a transcontinental railroad that would cross the Territory of Arizona along the thirty-fifth parallel between the Rio Grande and the Colorado River. The route essentially followed the survey of Lt. A. W. Whipple, who explored the region in December 1853.[5]

With the railroad's completion, the cattle industry in northern Arizona began to grow in the early 1880s. Chief among the large outfits was the Aztec Land and Cattle Company. Although the corporation bought one million acres from the Atlantic and Pacific

Brand and Mark of Aztec Cattle Co. Filed June 2nd 1885 10 O'clock a.m. Henry Warren and Records their Mark and Brand as follows. to wit: Hash Knife. on Both sides of cattle. same Brand on Left and Right shoulder of Horses. Ear Mark this

And now on this second day of June 1885. at 10 o'clock a.m. Comes the Aztec Cattle Company by their agent

Railroad, it actually received more than that for no additional charge. Some of the land, however, was occupied by cattlemen and sheepmen who had small prior land grants from the Spanish and Mexican governments that the U.S. government promised to recognize. Claims of ownership persisted until 1904, when the federal government was finally able to settle most of the disputes.[6]

The Aztec Land and Cattle Company had been formed in the Mills Building offices of the investment firm of J. & W. Seligman & Co. in New York on December 14, 1884, with a capital of $1 million. The first stock certificate, in the amount of 1,454 shares, was issued to J. & W. Seligman & Co. Additional capital was raised in Europe.[7]

By a contract of sale dated December 27, 1884, the land claimed by the company was sold by the railroad for $500,000 to Edward W. Kinsley, trustee for the subscribers to the capital stock of the cattle company. Three days later the land was released by the United States Trust Company, holder of the mortgage on railroad lands.[8]

On January 3, 1885, the Aztec Land and Cattle Company was formally organized in New York City, and officers were named by a group of Texas ranchers, J. & W. Seligman & Co., and stockholders of the Atlantic and Pacific Railroad Company who had released to the organization landholdings in Arizona for grazing purposes. Edward W. Kinsley, railroad commissioner of Massachusetts, was named president.[9]

Several sale contracts on the land purchased by the Aztec Land and Cattle Company were consummated over the first few years as a result of trusts that were found to have been sold, reserved, or

41

Stock Brand
Aztec Land & Cattle Co.

Know all persons by these presents, that the undersigned, the Aztec Land & Cattle Company has this day adopted the following as its Stock brand for Cattle & Horses.

I. Brand placed on Cattle, on both Sides of Animal, and on horses, brand is placed on left Shoulder of Animal — Ear Mark for Cattle is "Grub" the right

The stock so marked and branded, range at a point about eight miles North of Mormon Dairy, due East to the East Boundary line of the County, thence South to the South Boundary line of the A & P, R.R. grant, Thence west along the line to the S.W. corner, of Township 14. Range 9 — Thence North to place of beginning — in Yavapai County Arizona.

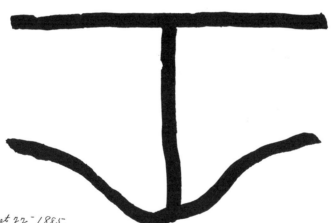

Dated August 22nd 1885,
      Aztec Land & Cattle Co. Sin
                  by Henry Warren — Gen Manager,
Recorded at request of Henry Warren Sept 28th A.D. 1885, at 9 O.clock A. M. in Book 3. of Marks & Brands at page 41. Records of Yavapai County Arizona —
                  William Wilkinson
                  County Recorder

occupied by homesteaders, preempted, or otherwise disposed of prior to the definite location of the Atlantic and Pacific Railroad.

In a revised contract, the purchase of the estimated 1,058,560 acres at the rate of fifty cents an acre was recorded in Apache County, Arizona, on February 3, 1886. It was described as every alternate section of public land, designated by odd numbers, to the amount of twenty sections a mile on each side of the railroad. Future revisions of the sale contract were said to be anticipated from surveys made, or to be made, by the United States.[10]

An area newspaper reported on June 18, 1885, that the huge land purchase was one of the most extensive ever made in the United States. It was also noted that the company received 1,125,000 acres and was allowed the privilege of selecting any section it chose, resulting in the control of nearly all watered sections of grazing land in northeast Arizona within the forty-mile limits of the railroad grant.[11]

Corporate executives of the vast northern Arizona cattle empire at ranch headquarters near St. Joseph (St. Joe, Joseph City, Joe City), west of Holbrook, included Captain Henry Warren, banker and cattleman from Weatherford, Texas, who became vice-president and general manager. E. J. Simpson, a Hash Knife executive in Texas and one of the founders of the new company, was named superintendent. Other resident executives were two young New England in-

Right: Edward James Simpson (1847–1910). (Courtesy of Jackie Simpson McLennan.) *Below:* Aztec Land and Cattle Company ranch buildings in 1886. Company official Henry Kinsley is on the horse in the left foreground. Behind him is the kitchen and dining house. The grain house is in the center of the photograph. On the right is the headquarters building and office. (National Archives, Washington, D.C.)

Frank A. Ames, his horse "Dandy," and Ed Rogers, Hash Knife wagon boss. Photograph by J. C. Burge, Flagstaff, Arizona. (National Archives, Washington, D.C.)

vestors whose families were closely associated with the railroad industry. Henry Kinsley, nephew of the company president, became assistant treasurer, and Frank A. Ames, grandson of railroad magnate Oakes Ames, became land agent.[12]

The newly formed Aztec Land and Cattle Company incurred an indebtedness of $330,000 with the purchase of around 32,000 head of cattle from the Continental Land and Cattle Company on April 23, 1885. The transaction included "the bands, droves and herds . . . running at large and being used . . . on the Pecos River" in the West Texas counties of Pecos and Reeves. All conveyed livestock and cattle were said to be branded "with what is called a hash-Knife."[13] In the summer of 1885, Charles W. Buster, who was in charge of Hash Knife operations on the Pecos River, turned over 34,000 cattle and some smaller individual herds to Henry Warren, manager of the new ranch.[14]

The transfer of Hash Knife cattle from West Texas to Arizona, by both trail and rail, began in the spring of 1885. Fifteen-year-old Son Collier was sent alone from the Pecos ranch up the trail to catch up with two Montana-bound Hash Knife herds with a message to divert the cattle west for delivery to the Aztec Land and Cattle Company.[15]

Subsequent trail herds had not arrived in the vicinity of Albuquerque by the last week in May, from which point they were to have been shipped in railroad cars to their destination in Holbrook.[16] By the first week in August, however, some Hash Knife cowboys were already in Arizona displaying their typical rowdiness when one almost killed a railroad worker during an altercation. A St. Johns newspaper warned its readers, "'Monkey' ye not with the festive cow boy, or your days will be short and full of trouble."[17]

Trail herds bound for the railhead near Albuquerque were made up along the west side of the Pecos and followed the river north into New Mexico Territory. Lead steers were pointed west near Fort Sumner, and the herds trailed to the Rio Grande. South of Albuquerque, the cattle were loaded into livestock cars and shipped to Arizona.[18]

On New Year's Day, 1886, an Albuquerque newspaper noted that Hash Knife cattlemen were guests at a local hotel: "A number of cattlemen from Pecos, Texas, are now at the San Felipe, having brought in a large herd of long-horns for the Aztec cattle company of Holbrook, Arizona. This company has recently purchased from the Atlantic & Pacific land department, a range consisting of a parcel of

Henry Kinsley, Hash Knife executive. (National Archives, Washington, D.C.)

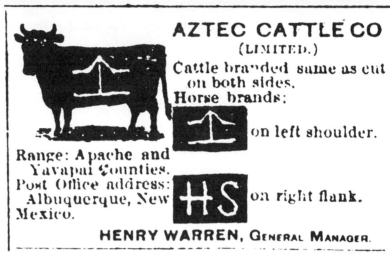

AZTEC CATTLE CO
(LIMITED.)

Cattle branded same as cut on both sides.
Horse brands:

on left shoulder.

Range: Apache and Yavapai Counties.
Post Office address: Albuquerque, New Mexico.

on right flank.

HENRY WARREN, General Manager.

Above: Headquarters of the Aztec Land and Cattle Company from the rear in 1886. The building in the left has the Hash Knife brand painted on the roof. (National Archives, Washington, D.C.)
Right: The first Hash Knife newspaper advertisement of the Aztec Land and Cattle Company, printed when the company offices were temporarily in Albuquerque, New Mexico. (*St. Johns* [Arizona Territory] *Herald,* June 11, 1885)

land ninety-five by forty-five miles with plenty of good water, and are now stocking it with forty thousand head of cattle."[19]

By the spring of 1886, those Hash Knife herds to be transferred from Texas entirely by rail were gathered wherever they were found on the west side of the Pecos River, loaded at Toyah, and then shipped to El Paso on the Texas and Pacific Railway. From there they were sent north on the Santa Fe Railway to Isleta, just south of Albuquerque, then west to Holbrook or Winslow on the line owned by the Atlantic and Pacific Railroad Company.

Hash Knife herds that were trailed all the way from Texas to northern Arizona went north along the Pecos into New Mexico, then west past the Sacramento Mountains to Tularosa. To the northwest a waterless stretch of trail, extending for a hundred miles, had to be negotiated before herds reached the Rio Grande opposite San Marcial. They crossed the river in the Socorro area, then trailed west by Magdalena to Springerville in the Arizona Territory. From

Looking west along the Atlantic and Pacific Railroad in Holbrook, Arizona Territory, before the disastrous fire in June 1888 that destroyed most of the buildings in town. (National Archives, Washington, D.C.)

there the herd was pointed northwest along the Little Colorado River to the new Hash Knife ranges.

During the early movement of cattle from Texas to Arizona, company business was transacted out of Albuquerque, but a permanent business office was soon established in Holbrook. Before the first Hash Knife cattle were due to arrive by train in Arizona, company official F. A. Ames wired the stationmaster in Holbrook to express all cowpunchers to Albuquerque on the next train. While trying desperately to round up all the cowboys he could find, it dawned on the agent that what was needed in Albuquerque were the long prod poles used to load and unload cattle. The "cowpunchers" were quickly dispatched.[20]

By late spring, trailing cattle from the Pecos was temporarily suspended because of continuing drought. The Arizona cattle journal *Hoof and Horn* reported on May 20, 1886: "E. J. Simpson, manager of the Aztec Cattle Company, came into Pecos, Texas, recently from up the river and gave a gloomy report about the herds that started on the trail via the Pecos river. He says they are scattered along the river from forty to a hundred miles and can not go any further, as both horses and cattle have become so poor and weak that they cannot travel, and are dying at a fearful rate. The drought still continues. Three thousand heads of cattle have already perished in the Pecos Valley."[21]

Cattle arrived in Arizona by rail throughout the summer of 1886. By the middle of June, the shipment from El Paso intensified in numbers and regularity. A local newspaper commented on the busy schedule: "On Wednesday and Thursday [June 16 and 17], the Santa Fe took out 28 cars of stock. E. J. Simpson, of the Aztec Cattle

Company, is sending 300 cars of stock to Winslow, A. T., over the Santa Fe, which will come up at the rate of two and three cars a day."[22]

During the final roundup of Hash Knife cattle on the Pecos range, W. D. (Bill) Casey, a struggling young rancher in the Davis Mountains, fifty miles southwest of Pecos City, asked the range boss of the vacating company if the Hash Knife brand was for sale. He was told to come back the following day and get the answer from the ranch manager. "He was there the next morning," according to Casey's son-in-law Joe Rounsaville, "and the Hash-knife Outfit sold him the brand for $350.00. He gathered 5,500 head of cattle out of it, and that's what put him on his feet."[23] Casey had moved to the Davis Mountains from the upper Rio Hondo in New Mexico where his father, Robert, was killed by a hired assassin on August 2, 1885, at the start of the bloody Lincoln County War.

By 1887 the number of Hash Knife cattle reaching Holbrook and Winslow from the Pecos totaled 17,000 by trail and another 23,000 by rail.[24]

Stocked with Hash Knife cattle from Texas, the Aztec Land and Cattle Company began operations in Apache and Yavapai counties

Will Croft Barnes (1856–1936), ranching neighbor of the Aztec Land and Cattle Company and a chronicler of the Hash Knife in Arizona. (*McClure's Magazine,* January 1909)

on its million-acre range laid off in a standard checkerboard division of odd- and even-numbered sections. No longer was it available to cattlemen and sheepmen who had formerly occupied it as free range. By owning alternate odd-numbered sections, the new company could prevent anyone else from crossing Hash Knife property to graze stock on the even-numbered sections of public lands. This left the Aztec Land and Cattle Company with exclusive rights to another million acres of free grazing land along the railroad right-of-way between Holbrook and Flagstaff.[25] The charge was made that Hash Knife cowboys threatened death to anyone who claimed even-numbered sections of government land that joined them or were located inside their range.[26]

Will C. Barnes, a native Californian, entered the cattle business on the Chevelon Fork of the Little Colorado River in the fall of 1883. When Texans began arriving in the area with the Aztec Land and Cattle Company two years later, they brought equipment and methods of working cattle that were strange to northern Arizona cowboys, used to California gear, techniques, and vocabulary. Barnes described the changes introduced by the newcomers:

They brought to us the first Rim-fire double-rigged saddles we had ever seen. We up that way were California center-fire men and used a 70 foot rawhide reata and all that sort of thing. These new boys with their double cinch saddles, grass ropes, "tied hard and fast to the nub," little old potmaker spurs and such new wrinkles surely taught us a whole lot about handling cows. They called us "Chaps, Taps, and Latigo Straps" in derision of our beloved California outfits. We watched them for a while and then, realizing the unwelcome fact that they knew more cow stuff in a week than we did in a year we quickly put away our cherished high horn single cinch California saddles and 70 ft. long reatas, bought us a Texas saddle, cached away the long flapping tapaderos we loved so much, bought a 35 ft. grass rope and tied it hard and fast, and soon forgot our previous training and accepted the new styles with all good graces.

Up to about 1887 we had no chuck wagon but were what the Texans called a "Greasy Sack Outfit," i.e., Pack. Each man came to the roundup with his own string of horses, his own rawhide hobbles which he had spent hours making during the long winter eve-

nings around the horse camp, and all his belongings packed on some old mare with a bell on her neck, and often with a colt following her.[27]

A group of roughshod cowboys and undesirables followed the Hash Knife stock to Arizona. Some were good men, but many were professional gunfighters. Others were fugitives who had drifted to the Arizona frontier because of criminal records in Texas and New Mexico. Rustling cattle from their employers and terrorizing Mormon settlers along the Little Colorado River became routine. A few took part in the Pleasant Valley War between cattlemen and sheepmen south of their range, even though it was not their fight. In the deadly conflict, also called the Tonto Basin War, waylaying and murder were practiced by both sides. A number of Hash Knife cowboys, potentially as dangerous and destructive as the brutal weapon burned on the hides of company cattle, sometimes acted as if they had been seared with the same hot iron. It became a stamp of violence and supportive of the fearsome designation earned by the company and its riders throughout the years—"the Hashknife outfit."[28]

Will C. Barnes described the untamed stock and his equally undisciplined neighbors: "Those Texas cattle could stand more grief, use less food, drink less water, and bear more calves than any cows that ever wore a brand. The owners also brought with them a bunch

A group of early Hash Knife cowboys in Holbrook. *Left to right:* Ed Rogers, John Taylor, Charlie Baldridge, Jim Burdette, F. A. Ames, Don McDonald, Bill Smith, and Tom Smith. (National Archives, Washington, D.C.)

of men of equal meanness, wildness, and ability to survive most anything in the way of hardships and sheriffs."[29]

Many early Hash Knife cowboys had to remain anonymous because of their pasts. Some volunteered a first name only, and more than likely it was not the right one. The code of the West was not to ask. So many Smiths worked for the company at one time that they were referred to as Smith A, Smith B, and so on, according to the order in which they came to work.

Jo Johnson (Baéza), who was raised in Holbrook and knew a few of the old-timers, explained some of the names and colorful epithets that individualized them without revealing their true identities: "Almost all the men had nicknames. Some served as aliases, some were merely to distinguish all the Bobs, Bills and Johns. Jeff White, a quick-witted fellow, usually christened the men. In 1890 a young cowboy named Johnny Paulsell came into camp, the last of many Johnnies to arrive. From that day on until he died he was 'Johnny-Come-Lately.' Names could almost tell the story of Arizona—they were wonderful names, like simple strong poetry of the West—Cap Warren, Pete Slaughter, Burr Williams, Mose Tate, 'Billy St. Joe,' 'Windy Bob' Stansel, 'Loco Tom' Lucky, 'Ace of Diamonds,' 'Poker Bill,' etc."[30]

Meager information on the names and backgrounds of the earliest Hash Knife boys was about all that was known. The piecemeal recollections of Lucien Creswell about fellow worker Billy Wilson are typical: "Billy wasn't called Billy because his name was William. It wasn't William but I don't recall what it was."[31] Creswell maintained that Wilson and Tom Pickett of the Hash Knife were the same Billy Wilson and Tom Pickett who rode with Billy the Kid a few years earlier in New Mexico. Although this was a common belief held by company cowboys and local residents at that time, the identities now appear to have been based on misinformation.

"Tom Tuck" was what the Mormons called Tom Tucker, the former Texan who held down the line shack at the water hole nearest the company headquarters. Although they tried, the Mormons never were successful in grazing their sheep near him.[32]

"Long Bill" distinguished one Bill from the others. Long Bill Jackson was tried in 1891 for attacking Mormon sheepmen at the Buckskin watering place above Heber. He was turned loose by a jury that had seven cowboys on it. A number of Hash Knife men besides Jackson—Bud Monger, Pink Burdett, Tom Flores, Henry Pruser, and Tom South—were remembered by Jim Pierce, a Mormon who had unfortunate dealings with all of them. Pruser was killed by Hook Larson, who in turn died a natural death.[33] Tom South was a cook. He made an unauthorized drive of some company cattle to Colorado where he sold them and opened up a saloon with the money from the sale. He went broke, returned to Arizona, and got another job with the Hash Knife.[34]

One of the many Jims who worked for the Hash Knife in later years rode a saddle equipped with a single cinch that hung down directly below the fork. This style of saddle rigging, known as a Spanish rig, rim-fire, or rimmy, was the reason he went by the name "Rimmy Jim" Giddings. His eventual residence and trading post, located five miles north of Meteor Crater, or Coon Hole, was identified on maps as Rimmy Jims, Arizona.

In the spring of 1886, immense herds of sheep from New Mexico were driven into Arizona to graze on the abundant grass and forage along the Little Colorado River and as far west as the San Francisco Mountains. According to Will C. Barnes, they advanced like an invading army on a front about ten miles wide with four separate bands on each side of the river. By the time Barnes became an active participant in resisting the incursion, "several fights had taken place already between sheepmen and cattlemen; sheep herds had been broken up and scattered all over the range; hundreds of sheep had been killed and injured; camps shot up; cattle killed on the range; herders beaten; and men killed on each side."[35]

In late March, the Aztec Land and Cattle Company began taking legal steps to stop the encroachment on company lands by "armed marauders, who, in nearly every instance, are not residents of the Territory."[36] By mid-June 1886, the courts were already prosecuting them for trespassing on Hash Knife ranges. The *St. Johns Herald* applauded the action at the same time it was trying to soothe the feelings between local cattle and sheep interests: "If both our cattle and sheep men were as active [as the courts] in ridding the country of these New Mexico sheep, a better feeling would exist between our home stockmen who represent the different stock interests. These wandering herds not only eat out the range of our cattlemen, but eat out the range that of right belongs to our citizens who are engaged in raising sheep."[37]

Transient New Mexico sheep overrunning Apache County ranges at this time were estimated to number at least 150,000 head. There were also 120,000 resident sheep. Apache County cowboy Albert F. Potter, who later became the county treasurer, wrote, "This resulted in a sheep and cattle war, which finally culminated in the Tonto Basin War of 1887."[38] The annual illegal migration of New Mexico sheep herds into northern Arizona lasted until about 1890.

On the seemingly boundless Hash Knife ranges and the small Mormon homesteads, unbranded stock past weaning age was fair game to anyone. A saddle horse and a long rope were said to be all that was needed to get a start in the cattle business.[39] Brand altering became a science in northern Arizona.

Small ranchers prospered by branding mavericks, and some Hash Knife workers took calves the same way. The constant fear of their own past being exposed kept most of the cowboys quiet about any rustling within the company. Others simply did not want to turn in fellow workers.

A popular method of stealing cattle from the Aztec Land and Cattle Company was to convert unbranded calves into what were known on the range as "sleepers." When rustlers found a new Hash Knife calf with its mother, they put the appropriate company earmarks on it and turned it loose unbranded. Seeing the earmarked calf at roundup time, Hash Knife cowboys often assumed, either innocently or intentionally, that the calf had also been range branded and left it alone. The patient rustler would return later and replace the Hash Knife earmarks with new ones that surgically destroyed those made earlier. Then he applied his own brand to the calf.[40]

Another way to steal company cattle was to mark calves by cutting their hair away neatly from the flesh in the shape of a Hash Knife brand, giving the appearance of a brand that had healed. By the time the "haircut" grew out, the calf would be classed as a maverick and marked by the rustler with his own brand. Other calves were "hair branded" with a Hash Knife iron, which meant scorching the hair away with enough care not to scar the flesh. The hair came back the same as if the design had been trimmed with a knife. The animals were then rebranded by thieves.

A further variation of the illegal scheme was recalled by an area resident: "Another trick they had was to have part of the Hash-Knife brand as their own, which part they would brand deep into the hide, the other part of the Hash-Knife brand was just placed deep enough to burn, so when the hair grew again the only brand visible was that of the outlaw cowboys. So that not only the Mormon colonists, but the Aztec Land & Cattle Company lost heavily."[41]

On November 20, 1886, officials of the Apache County Stock Association, meeting in St. Joseph, Arizona, adopted a "mistake brand" to be used when returning calves branded through error or when an owner chose not to vent brand, that is, invalidate one brand with another, which would indicate a sale or change of ownership. Cattlemen were directed to place an M brand on the right side of the neck of the illegally branded calves as well as on the ones given in return.[42]

At times, a cow thief would burn a newly devised brand on an unmarked Hash Knife calf, in addition to an M on the neck or shoulder. If company cowboys took for granted the correction had already been made and left the animal alone, the calf was later appropriated by the rustler. An Irishman named Dan Mahoney is said to have registered his own initials for a brand, and when he found a calf marked with an M, he simply added a D in front of it and claimed the animal.[43]

Even though the Hash Knife brand was difficult to alter, some attempted to change it. Will Barnes told of one case in which the mark was added to until it looked like the head of a cow drinking out of a watering trough. A few of the brand-doctored animals attracted immediate attention at one of the spring roundups because the marks were so unusual. A suspicious Hash Knife foreman was positive he could detect the company brand disguised in the new one. He proposed that one of the animals be killed and skinned; if the inside of the hide did not clearly reveal the older Hash Knife brand, he would pay double the value of the animal. When the animal was skinned in the presence of a brand inspector and other witnesses, the Hash Knife brand stood out clearly and distinctly on the inside

of the hide. The only defense of the claimant was his testimony "I was just a-funnin'." His fun cost him several years in prison.[44]

With a mandate to combat the prevailing lawlessness of well-organized outlaw gangs, wild cowboys, corrupt county officials, and a range war over grazing rights, Commodore Perry Owens, a drifting cowboy with the reputation of a gunfighter, was elected sheriff by the reform element of Apache County in 1886. It was not long until he saved the lives of two Hash Knife cowboys.

Tom Pickett and another cowboy known only as Peck, short for the fictional "Peck's Bad Boy" in American literature, were on their way to Holbrook on April 7, 1887, but stopped and spent the night at the ranch of Will Barnes. The next day, the rancher accompanied them to town. He went to bed early that night at the Apache Hotel, but the cowboys proceeded to get liquored up. Then they barged in on a Mexican dance at the schoolhouse.[45] An area newspaper reported on the tense atmosphere created by the intrusion of the cowboys: "As usual some of the 'caballeros' thought the Americans were monopolizing the 'senoritas' and took umbrage thereat."[46]

The difficulties inside were confined to words. But plenty of action broke out later on the street in front of the bakery. Some thirty

Commodore Perry
Owens, Apache County
sheriff, 1887–88.
(Photo no. 6265, Ari-
zona Historical Society
Library, Tucson)

to forty shots were exchanged in rapid succession between the two cowboys and a number of Mexicans. Angel Benajos was killed with three gunshots in the heart and stomach.

Pickett was shot in the ankle. The bullet ranged downward and passed through his foot diagonally, but the cowboy made it back to the hotel, where the landlady dressed his wound. A group of Mexicans bent on revenge were about to storm the hotel the next morning when Sheriff Owens rode into town and dispersed them.[47] Pickett's right leg had to be amputated much later as a result of the fray.

During the blood feud between the Grahams and Tewksburys in Pleasant Valley, south of the Mogollon Rim, some of the turmoil extended north into Hash Knife ranges. Cattle rustling and lawlessness went virtually unchecked in northeast and east-central Arizona. One contemporary Mormon source gave the astounding figure of 52,000 head of cattle unlawfully branded in one year by outlaw cowboys, some of whom worked for the Hash Knife.[48]

In June 1887, Martin J. ("Old Man") Blevins left his house on Canyon Creek, just south of the Mogollon Rim, to look for horses. He never returned. Suspecting foul play, his sons and confederates organized a search party, split up, and headed in different directions. Hamp Blevins and Robert Carrington rode northeast and met up with Hash Knife cowboys John Paine, Tom Tucker, and Bob Gillespie, who joined forces with them.

Blevins and his new allies rode into a roundup camp at Big Dry Lake, thirty miles south of Holbrook, on August 3. The men spent the night and left early the next morning. According to Ed Rogers, a Hash Knife wagon boss, the riders were headed for Pleasant Valley to find out what they could about the disappearance of Old Man Blevins and, as one of them put it, "start a little war of our own."[49] What happened over the next five days is not known. Some accounts say the group stopped by the Graham ranch and doubled their numbers.

On August 9, the armed band arrived at the old Middleton cabin a few miles southeast of the Graham ranch. They were surprised to find sheepmen Ed and Jim Tewksbury and several supporters temporarily housed in the vacant cabin. Following a heated exchange of words between the two factions, a deadly volley of gunfire from the cabin toppled four of the five cowboys from their saddles. In this opening battle of the Pleasant Valley War, Blevins and Paine were dead before they hit the ground, and Tucker and Gillespie were seriously wounded. Carrington managed to escape in a hail of bullets.[50] For some time it was thought that Tucker and Gillespie had not survived the shootout, but they both crawled to safety despite serious wounds. Two weeks later, an Apache County newspaper explained the reason for the Hash Knife cowboys being on the prowl:

> *The three men reported killed in Tonto Basin, Tucker, Gillespie and Payne [sic], had been in the employ of the Aztec Cattle Company for some time. We understand that Mr. Simpson, the local manager, had determined to do all in his power to break up the band of horse and cattle thieves who had been preying on the people in the western part of this county for so long a time, and to that end called all the men together in the employ of that company. When they were assembled he told them it was the intention of the company to take an active part in trying to stop so much stealing, and wanted the help of all the employees of the company—that those who were not willing to assist them and the authorities in this work, could call for their time. All agreed to do what they could except five, who took their money and left. The three above named were of the party who took their time. It appears they put their liberty to bad use and enjoyed it but a short time.[51]*

Cattle rustling and death threats against them were foremost on the minds of Executive Committee members of the Apache County Stock Association when they gave specific instructions through Ben Irby to cowboys of the various ranches in the county before the fall rodeo (roundup) of 1887: "Brand every calf you can, no matter to whom it belongs. This Association proposes to put a stop to 'mavericking' if it can be done, and the Committee believes that by branding every calf found, it will greatly decrease the number of mavericks, and thus lessen the temptation to steal."[52] Roundup bosses for the six designated sections in the county were told to keep careful records of such brands and tallies, and motherless calves with no owners were to be advertised in the newspaper. The bosses were further instructed to forbid all horse racing and gambling.

The Hash Knife crew was assigned to work its own ranges: "From Woodruff . . . down the [Little Colorado] river, Mr. Ed. Rogers will take charge. At Holbrook, Mr. Rodgers [sic] will divide his party, sending an outfit up the Puerco to, and beyond if necessary, Bennett's ranch; thence swing round by Tanner Springs, working the Leroux wash, over the X ranges, then down the Cottonwood to its mouth, joining the other party at Clear Creek. The remainder of Mr. Roger's outfit will work down the river to Clear Creek, where, after joining party No. 1 the entire outfit will work back between the creeks to the Verde road, then east through the mountains, via Wilford, Phoenix Park and the Indian Tanks to Show Low."[53]

Henry Smith was in charge of the roundup crew at the Meadows, a lush grassland bordering the Little Colorado a few miles north of St. Johns. He also had an undisclosed assignment that resulted from a wave of serious crimes in the county for which no one had been convicted. Smith, an Englishman and owner of the Twenty-Four Cattle Company, was president of the Apache County Stock Association at the time. He had been given the authority, under utmost secrecy, to hire a "range detective" with orders to rid the county of thieves and cutthroats. Only he and Will Barnes, secretary of the organization, knew who the contact was. The covert activities of the hired gunman were cold, calculated, and swift. Two of the worst characters in the county were "killed while resisting arrest" a few days after he was hired. He shot first, with no questions asked, and then read warrants over the dead bodies. The undercover assassin broke up a number of outlaw gangs before he disappeared as quietly as he had arrived to take a similar assignment in California.[54]

Less than a year after Commodore Perry Owens was elected sheriff of Apache County, he was immortalized in a one-minute drama that unfolded at midafternoon on September 4, 1887, in a western gunfight that one writer says deserves to be called "astounding."[55]

Sheriff Owens went alone to a cottage north of the railroad tracks in Holbrook to arrest a known outlaw, Andy Blevins, alias Andy Cooper, who had boasted of killing two men only two days earlier. Unknown to the sheriff, two of Blevins's brothers and another adult male, sometimes identified as a relative, were with him inside. Owens approached the dwelling in full view of the armed men holed up in the comparative safety of the house. His call for the surrender of the suspect was refused, and a shootout erupted. A minute later, Owens walked away from the scene unscathed, leaving three men dead or dying and the other wounded.[56]

Typically, the deadly gunplay and escapades of some Hash Knife cowboys in town or anywhere else continued to overshadow the legitimate pursuit of tending cattle for their company. John Taylor, regarded as a "holy terror," was one of them. On December 8, 1887, Taylor rode his horse onto the portico in front of Page's saloon in Winslow, waving his pistol and swearing vengeance against someone inside who had offended him. The *St. Johns Herald* described his last mistake: "While he was still ranting, he rode up to a window and was looking in, when some one on the inside shot him—the shot taking effect in the forehead." A coroner's jury ruled that "the deceased came to his death from a gunshot wound in the hands of some unknown party."[57]

At least two more Hash Knife cowboys, James Scott and Billy Wilson, were to perish in the disorder identified with the bloody range feud in Pleasant Valley, which is conservatively estimated to have caused thirty casualties and perhaps as many as fifty.[58] They were unknowingly in the wrong place at the wrong time. Scott was originally from Weatherford, Texas. In Arizona he was a bog rider for the Hash Knife on Silver River between Snowflake and the Little Colorado River. Wilson, also called Jeff Wilson, was a wagon cook for the company. The two cowboys, who may have been involved in illegal activities, were murdered, along with James Stott, near Stott's ranch.

Massachusetts native James W. Stott owned the Circle Dot ranch at Bear Springs, some sixty miles south of Holbrook, and was a close friend of Hash Knife official F. A. Ames, who came from the same state. Stott supposedly made the mistake of trading for some horses that had blotched brands, brands that had been "worked over" into other brands. Tragically, for Scott and Wilson, they were at the Stott ranch when a posse arrived before breakfast on August 11, 1888, with a warrant charging the ranch owner with horse stealing. The posse decided to take Scott and Wilson also into custody. Its leader, James D. Houck, Tewksbury partisan and part-time lawman, had little regard for Scott, anyway, since the Hash Knife cowboy had backed him down in an argument one night in Holbrook. The

lifeless bodies of Stott, Scott, and Wilson were later found hanging from a large ponderosa pine not far from the ranch.[59]

Houck had previously threatened and intimidated Stott in an attempt to take possession of his ranch before Stott "proved up" his claim. Stott was due to receive a clear title to the homestead during the upcoming month. After the murders, Houck circulated an unfounded story that the victims had taken shots at three different men. He easily convinced officials that outlaws had taken his prisoners and lynched them.[60] A story out of Holbrook, dateline August 16, 1888, noted the judicial complacency of local officials:

Reports from Pleasant Valley of the lynching, by outlaws, of James Stott, James Scott, and Jeff Wilson, near Stott's ranch, on the afternoon of the 11th, received here up to date are as follows: The parties were arrested on alleged ficticious charges, and were in charge of Jas. D. Houck and five others. They were en route to Pleasant Valley, and when near the Canyon Creek trail were met by masked men who ordered Houck and his men to move on. The prisoners were found next morning hanging near the Verde road. Houck arrived in Holbrook on Monday, August [13th], and the latest intelligence from the scene was on Tuesday morning, when the bodies were reported as still hanging. From the best information today the county authorities are taking no action in the matter.[61]

Things appeared to be looking good for the Aztec Land and Cattle Company in the spring of 1888, despite the heavy loss of cattle to rustlers and cowboys to violence. Company official Henry Kinsley made an extensive tour of the leading cities of California and Mexico by rail in the "private palace car" of his uncle, the company president.[62] The Hash Knife was also running 60,000 head of cattle in northern Arizona during the year.[63]

E. J. Simpson, who had supervised the moving of Hash Knife cattle from the Pecos, returned to Texas in the summer of 1888 to bring his wife, sister, and newborn son to their home in Arizona. The "first class boy," as he was described in his birth announcement in the St. Johns *Apache Review*,[64] lived up to the preliminary assessment. In 1944, as General William Hood Simpson, he became commander of the Ninth Army in Europe, one of the most distinguished fighting units in American military history.

In addition to bringing back members of his family, the father of the future hero returned to Arizona with a trail herd identified as "the remnants of the cattle brought from Texas last year and year before."[65] The herd arrived on the company range near Holbrook in mid-August 1888 in excellent condition. The drive was one of the most successful ever taken by the company. The *Apache Review* commented, "Mr. E. J. Simpson, the popular manager for the Aztec Cattle Company, recently drove 2,000 head of cattle from Weatherford, Texas, to Holbrook, at a cost of only 75 cents per head, and with a loss of only six animals in making the journey. By doing this he saved nearly $5,000 for his company."[66]

The economic success of this trail drive was insignificant, however, compared to the company's staggering annual operational losses, partly attributable to rustlers. Yet, the following year, the

Aztec Land and Cattle Company shipped twenty-eight carloads of two-year-olds from Holbrook to Kansas by rail.[67]

Mormon losses to rustlers were also heavy. The family of J. D. Pierce had been the first to settle on Silver Creek in Apache County. In 1889 Pierce wrote to the secretary of the interior describing the deplorable range conditions that, he claimed, were created by the Hash Knife outfit. He also cited various offenses said to have been committed by company cowboys. Some Mormons retaliated by grazing their sheep on Hash Knife ranges and confiscating company cattle and horses under the pretense of getting back at the "robber barons" for beating honest, hard-working people out of their rights.[68] The Hash Knife built a line of cabin camps from the Mogollon Rim almost to within sight of Holbrook where tough men, reported to have been hired by Superintendent Simpson, were stationed to keep sheep and Mormon raiders off company property.

Lucien Creswell was a Hash Knife cowboy who helped drive an early herd from the Brazos River in Baylor County, Texas, to Las Vegas, New Mexico, where they were loaded into railroad cars and shipped to Holbrook. He claimed that Billy Wilson and Tom Pickett were purposely hired to pack guns and protect the cattle ranges. Another hired gunman he identified was Dave Rudabaugh, a former Billy the Kid associate in New Mexico, who went by the name Don Hill in Arizona. He was stationed at the Chevelon Buttes camp when Creswell renewed acquaintance with him, having first known the gunman in the Kansas cattle-shipping towns. According to Creswell, Rudabaugh hired on with the Hash Knife at Obed, the site of an early Mormon fort two miles south of Aztec headquarters. He worked on the east line at a cabin with Billy Wilson but moved from place to place whenever and wherever trouble erupted.[69]

At the Mormons' request, federal men were sent to St. Johns, Heber, Pleasant Valley, Holbrook, and other centers of lawlessness to investigate Mormon charges against the fearsome cowboys of the giant corporation. The fact-finding group reportedly went to the Hash Knife headquarters after the investigation and told "Cap" Warren to get rid of the "renegades" in his crew and never to hire them again.[70]

The boredom of inaction at the Hash Knife ranch during the winter of 1888 made it seem to some of the cowboys that spring roundup would never arrive. Many of them were broke. They played poker with unredeemable beans and stag-danced with each other while Jack Diamond played the fiddle.

Dan Harvick stood outside the door of the ranch house one evening and watched the sun go down in the direction of Sunset Pass. It seemed to him to go down forever, and he decided to try to relieve the monotony. He turned to Jack Smith and suggested they rob a train to spark up their lives and make names for themselves. "I'm tired of working day and night through the spring, and summer, and fall, stealing cattle for someone else and then waiting all winter for the chance to do it all over again," he reasoned.[71] William Sterin and John Halford joined the conversation outside. Before the four went back inside, they had agreed on a plan.

At 11 o'clock on the night of Wednesday, March 20, 1889, the little depot at Canyon Diablo was the scene of one of the most noted train robberies in the history of the West. Eastbound Number 7 of the Atlantic and Pacific Railroad Company was held up by the four Hash Knife cowboys when it stopped to replenish the woodbox. The Flagstaff paper reported a loss of between $700 and $800 and added that the men had overlooked a safe said to contain between $125,000 and $150,000.[72]

After receiving news of the robbery, Sheriff Buckey O'Neill of Yavapai County and his deputy, James L. Black, were joined by Special Deputy Ed St. Clair of Flagstaff and Carl Holton, a special agent with the Atlantic and Pacific Railroad, and the hunt was on. The outlaws' trail led north to the Little Colorado, crossed the river at Grand Falls, and continued on north through the heart of the Painted Desert. When the posse reached the crossing of the Big Colorado at Lee's Ferry, they were told the fugitives were two days ahead of them. They also learned that the robbers were headed for Wahweap Canyon and a Mormon settlement near Cannonville, Utah. Here the trail doubled back toward Arizona, but before the outlaws reached Lee's Ferry on the return trip, the sheriff and his posse had rounded them up.

Sheriff O'Neill loaded his prisoners on a wagon and drove to Milford, Utah, where the party boarded a train for Salt Lake City. After requisition papers were secured there, the prisoners were taken to Denver, then south toward New Mexico in a long, round-

The Canyon Diablo posse
that captured the Atlan-
tic and Pacific train robbers in 1889. *Left to
right:* Carl Holton, Jim
Black, Sheriff Buckey
O'Neill, and E. A. (Ed)
St. Clair. (Sharlot Hall
Historical Society, Pres-
cott, Arizona)

about return that would eventually take them back to Arizona. Jack Smith, the smallest of the robbers, found that if he pulled off one of his boots, the shackle around his ankle would come off with it. As the train crawled toward the summit of Raton Pass, Smith raised the window and jumped to temporary freedom. He was later recaptured in Texas. In Prescott the four robbers pled guilty. Three were given twenty-five years each in the Territorial Prison in Yuma, and Jack Smith received thirty years.

The amount of money taken from the train has remained a mystery. The men were said to have escaped with an undisclosed sum of gold coins that have not been found to this day. These coins are the basis of the many stories about hidden treasure in Canyon Diablo. Popular belief is that the loot was buried somewhere on the rim or down in the gorge near Two Guns.[73] One of the robbers said they took $7,000 out of one safe along with considerable jewelry.[74]

Sheriff Buckey O'Neill, who caught the robbers and followed the

Canyon Diablo bridge soon after its completion in 1883. (Santa Fe Railway, Schaumburg, Illinois)

case through their conviction, said that the robbery involved the greatest amount of money taken in the history of the Southwest. Buckey was offered $25,000 by the express company if he could find out what happened to the loot. In addition, each of the holdup men was offered a ticket to freedom and $10,000 for the same information before their trial began in Prescott.

Why the express company and railroad officials kept the exact amount secret no one ever knew. No records were produced to show the amount. One official, under oath, stated that the loss was about $25,000. Another in Albuquerque stated that he signed for $40,000, and still another swore the loss was between $30,000 and $45,000. Old-time cowman Bill Roden of Canyon Diablo, a personal friend of the Yavapai County sheriff, related the following conversation with him:

> *I said, "Bucky [sic], you mean there really was a lot of money taken by those ex-Hashknife cowboys? Maybe more than $50,000.*

Maybe over a $100,000?" That is as near as I ever came to asking him the amount.

"You aren't any ways near the right amount," he replied.

It was known, however, that officials of the express company at the trial did not wish to see the outlaws hang or be put in the pen too long. They believed that if none of the robbers would reveal where the gold was hidden, perhaps they could be trailed after their release from prison.[75]

None of the robbers served his full prison term. All were pardoned at varying intervals within seven years. According to Dan Harvick, one of the holdup men, William Sterin, was allowed to enlist in the Rough Riders under another name—his real one—for service in the Spanish-American War and was then released from prison. He was killed on San Juan Hill shortly after Buckey O'Neill, his former captor in the Arizona train robbery and commanding officer in Cuba, had met the same fate on July 1, 1898.[76]

Hash Knife official E. J. Simpson was elected "without any exertion on his part" to serve one term as the Democrats' representative from Apache County in the Arizona Territorial Assembly in 1889.[77] He continued as the Hash Knife ranch and range manager until the following year, when he divested himself of all business in the company. His wife, the former Elizabeth Hood of Weatherford, Texas, later recalled, "Sad to relate that his life savings, invested in the Aztecs, was a complete loss."[78]

Rustlers still plagued the northern Arizona ranges in the 1890s, but during his one term in office Sheriff Owens had done much to rid Apache County of organized outlaws. He alone almost wiped out the Blevins gang in one day, and his deputies killed or captured what was left of the notorious Clantons who had moved their field of operation from Tombstone to Springerville following the Earp-Clanton gunfight at the O K Corral. Carrying warrants that charged members of the family with cattle rustling in Apache County, J. V. ("Rawhide Jake") Brighton crossed over into Graham County and killed Ike Clanton on the headwaters of Eagle Creek on June 1, 1887.[79] Phineas Clanton was later captured and returned to St. Johns, convicted of cattle rustling, and sent to prison for ten years.[80]

Stock Brand.

Know all Men by these Presents:

That Aztec Land & Cattle Co, Limited, have adopted and do declare the following to be their Stock Brand for Cattle and Horses,

Cattle are branded as above on the Left ribs.

Horses are branded as above on the Left shoulder.

Ear mark for Cattle is: Crop off Right ear, Seven under bit in Left ear.

Range: Coconino County, Arizona Territory.

Post Office address; Holbrook, Navajo County, Arizona.
Dated, October 12th 1895.

Aztec Land & Cattle Co, Limited.
By John T. Jones.

Recorded October 12th, 1895.

A. Bush, County Recorder.

A brother-in-law, Erbin Stanley, was involved in the same case and given sixty days to leave the territory.[81]

When Apache County was divided in 1895 and Navajo County created out of the western half, Hash Knife offices, headquarters, and a major part of their range lay in the new county. John T. Jones, company manager, recorded the Hash Knife brand on October 12, 1895, in neighboring Coconino County,[82] which had been created in 1891 out of Yavapai County. By then, a seven underbit on the left ear had been added as a Hash Knife earmark in addition to a crop on the right ear instead of almost cutting it off completely as denoted, years earlier, in Yavapai County.[83] On February 18, 1897, the same brand and earmarks were recorded in Navajo County by the Aztec Land and Cattle Company.[84]

Overstocking the ranges was a major problem in northern Arizona in the mid-1890s. In 1895, instead of one cow to every one hundred acres—normally considered a fully stocked range—there were twenty cows on the same amount of land.[85] The dry years of 1895–96 were also disastrous for the Hash Knife outfit. Overstating enough to get his point across, one old-timer lamented, "By 1897 you couldn't have made a bale of hay if you had gathered up every blade of grass within a hundred miles of Holbrook."[86]

Western writer Dane Coolidge wrote extensively about early Arizona cowboys and interviewed men who worked for the early Hash Knife outfit, as well as other residents in the area during the troubled years. He found that renegade Mormons, Mexicans, and Hash Knife cowboys who had either quit or been fired had been engaged in stealing company cattle, with annual losses to the Aztec Land and Cattle Company of around $150,000. According to Coolidge, many observers believed that the major losses were caused by the firing of the first group of Hash Knife cowboys hired by the Arizona-based company. "Rightly or wrongly," he wrote, "the original Texas cowboys were accused of hair-branding calves and starting a little iron of their own. A big crew of men was sent down from Montana and the old men were given their time. Right there the trouble began. The first Texans moved back into the hills, where they went into business for themselves, and while the Montana men were getting settled down they branded every maverick in sight. Thus started the Hash-knife War, one of the greatest rustler wars in the West." But

Opposite: Hash Knife brand and earmarks recorded on October 12, 1895, in Coconino County, Arizona Territory. (*Record of Marks & Brands 1,* Coconino County, Arizona Territory, p. 273)

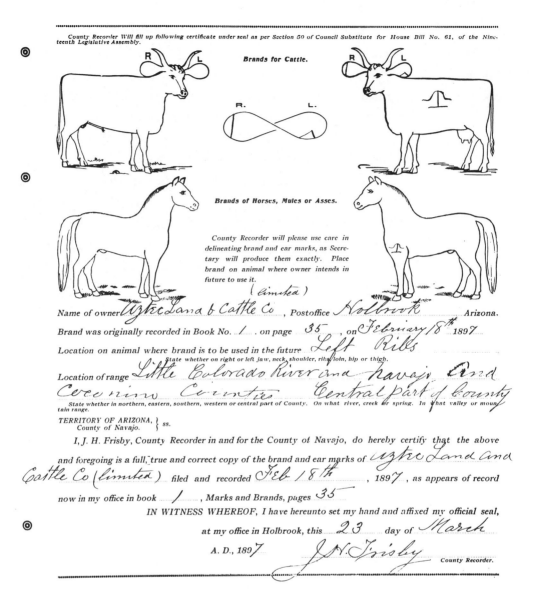

Brands for Cattle.

R.   L.

Brands of Horses, Mules or Asses.

County Recorder will please use care in delineating brand and ear marks, as Secretary will produce them exactly. Place brand on animal where owner intends to use it.

(limited)

Name of owner *Aztec Land & Cattle Co*, Postoffice *Holbrook* Arizona.

Brand was originally recorded in Book No. *1*. on page *35*, on *February 18th* 1897.

Location on animal where brand is to be used in the future *Left Ribs*
State whether on right or left jaw, neck, shoulder, ribs, loin, hip or thigh.

Location of range *Little Colorado River and Navajo And Coconino Counties Central part of County*
State whether in northern, eastern, southern, western or central part of County. On what river, creek or spring. In what valley or mountain range.

TERRITORY OF ARIZONA, } ss.
County of Navajo.

I, J. H. Frisby, County Recorder in and for the County of Navajo, do hereby certify that the above and foregoing is a full, true and correct copy of the brand and ear marks of *Aztec Land and Cattle Co (limited)* filed and recorded *Feb 18th*, 1897, as appears of record now in my office in book *1*, Marks and Brands, pages *35*.

IN WITNESS WHEREOF, I have hereunto set my hand and affixed my official seal, at my office in Holbrook, this *23* day of *March* A. D., 189*7*

J. H. Frisby
County Recorder.

Aztec Land and Cattle Company brand and earmarks, recorded in Navajo County. (*Territorial Brand Book*, entered May 1, 1897, Phoenix, Arizona Territory, p. 11)

that was not the end of company troubles, according to Coolidge. "Then," he continued, "the second gang of cow-hands went into business on their own account while still in Hash-knife employ, those with the east wagon gathering mavericks and shoving them west and the west wagon-crew pushing as many more east. A kind of pool had been formed among the cowboys themselves and they were stealing the Company blind."[87]

Desperately in need of tough new management, the Aztec Land and Cattle Company hired Burton C. Mossman, former cowboy and ranchman, who had run a large spread in New Mexico and for four

years had been superintendent of Thatcher Bros. & Bloom on their stock ranges in the Bloody Basin area of Arizona. His biographer, Frazier Hunt, summed up the urgent problems of the Aztec Land and Cattle Company that faced the new superintendent: "For fourteen years the outfit had paid no dividends on either stock or bonds, but it had won the unsavory reputation of harboring more outlaw cowboys, more thieving hands and murderous neighbors, than any ranch in the country. Rustlers and horse thieves were as thick as fleas on a dog's back. It still ran around fifty thousand head of cattle and a couple thousand horses."[88]

Mossman arrived in Holbrook on January 20, 1898, replacing John T. Jones as superintendent of the Hash Knife. He caught his first cattle thieves before he reported to headquarters. Upon his arrival, he was informed by Hash Knife cowboy Charlie Fought, who had been sent to meet him, that rustlers had just stolen a number of company cattle and were headed south toward Snowflake. Mossman and the cowboy rode in pursuit, captured the three thieves, and recovered the stolen property. Obviously impressed by the new company boss, Navajo County Sheriff Frank Wattron deputized him when he returned to Holbrook.[89]

One of Mossman's first company decisions was to clean out existing management and reduce the complement of eighty-four cowboys
on the payroll. On February 1, 1898, only ten days after his arrival,
he fired ranch manager Bob Morris and fifty-two cowboys who were
suspected of misdeeds. In place of the six to eight men who hung
around each of the eight company line camps, the new superintendent put two cowboys in each camp.[90]

Hash Knife cowboy Frank Wallace and 1,800 head of horses had
come to the company when the Waters Cattle Company, located on
the Clear Creek and Chevelon Fork ranges, sold out to the Aztec
Land and Cattle Company in 1896.[91] He had also worked with
Mossman in New Mexico. Wallace was appointed Hash Knife foreman at $75 a month. Mossman also named Pete Pemberton boss of
the west wagon crew that gathered cows between Winslow and Flagstaff. Pemberton had been imported earlier from Texas by Hash
Knife officials during a prolonged armed conflict with sheepmen.

Some 16,000 Hash Knife steers were shipped north and east in
1898. The company also had secured an Indian contract to supply
beef for the San Carlos Indian Reservation in Arizona. An initial 400
head of cattle were trailed over a hundred miles to the southeast by
veteran Hash Knife cowboy Barney Stiles and three more cowboys,
a cook, a wrangler, and six pack mules. The trail led from the
Mormon Lake range over the timbered escarpment of the Mogollon
Rim and on to Ash Creek through the rugged canyons and draws
that hem in the White and Black rivers.[92]

In June and July 1898, the east wagon crew and the west wagon
crew each branded 200 calves a day. The tally often ran as high as
400. The total for the two months was 16,000. Also eleven men were
in jail charged with rustling.[93]

During the fall term of court in Holbrook, the Hash Knife attorney publicly appealed to the Mormon bishops that it would be in the
interest of the church if Mormon renegades were convicted by Mormon juries for a change. Before the day ended, eleven cases, some
involving Mormon defendants, had been tried and eleven rustlers
sent to prison for terms ranging from two to four years. For the first
time in the fourteen-year history of the Aztec Land and Cattle Company, guilty verdicts had been returned against rustlers.[94]

A December snowstorm struck northern Arizona in 1898. Two

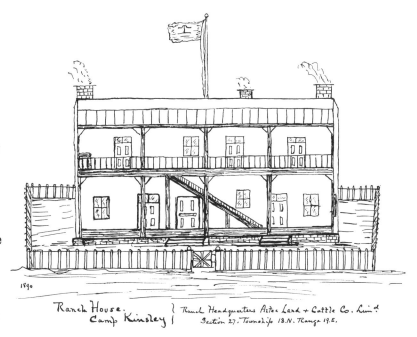

Above: Adobe brick headquarters of the Aztec Land and Cattle Company west of Holbrook, Arizona Territory, in the late 1890s. (Courtesy of Margaret Riseley Barbour.) *Right:* Drawing of the planned adobe headquarters building of the Aztec Land and Cattle Company built in 1890 on the original headquarters site, south of the Little Colorado River and opposite the Mormon town of St. Joseph, Arizona Territory. (Aztec Land and Cattle Company, Ltd., Mesa, Arizona)

feet of snow covered the Hash Knife ranges for ten straight weeks, and 10,000 head of cattle perished.[95] The company appeared to be doomed.

In addition to the bad weather and a bleak outlook for the future of the Aztec Land and Cattle Company, Mossman continued to round up rustlers whenever he received information on their activ-

ities. Perhaps the cruelest one he dealt with was Bill Young, a renegade Mormon who lived outside company property north of St.
Joseph and the Little Colorado. Young would cut out a block of hide
that carried the Hash Knife brand and sew the open ends together.
"It made a mean-looking scar that was proof enough of stealing, but
it wouldn't stand up in a court of law" is the way Mossman explained it to his biographer. Mossman took Young to trial for the
offense on two different occasions, but the rustler won both times.
After the second trial, Young announced that he was moving to
Colorado because he was being persecuted. There, he and his oldest
son were both sent to prison for twenty years for killing a man in
a row.[96]

Thieves were beginning to believe the safest way to steal Hash
Knife cattle was to hide company cows and their calves on the
southern edge of the Hash Knife range, which was covered with
stands of pine and cedar and contained an infinite number of hidden
canyons and secluded valleys. They branded the calves with im-
proper markings, penned them up, and ran off the mothers.

Hash Knife chuck wagons in Holbrook, Arizona Territory, at the time cattle were being shipped in June 1899. The wagon on the left was called the "east wagon," the one on the right the "west wagon." (J. & W. Seligman & Co. Archives, Bass Business Collection, University of Oklahoma, Norman)

This rustling technique was proved in one court case involving three thieves who were found guilty and sentenced to three years each in prison. In late spring 1899, near a small canyon in the wooded hill country east of Snowflake, Mossman and Deputy Joe Bargman found the rustlers' holding pens, which contained calves with fresh outlaw brands. The rustlers were arrested and returned to Holbrook. "Within an hour," according to Mossman, "Joe led Frank Wallace and a reliable witness back to the canyon and turned loose the freshly branded calves. They followed them until they located their mothers. Then they drove the bunch back to the county seat and put them in a corral. Several more witnesses were called in to see the calves, with their tell-tale brands, peacefully sucking the old Hash Knife cows."[97]

Even though Mossman showed a company profit for the first time by cutting back expenses and by sending cattle thieves to the territorial prison in Yuma, the company's cattle operation was about to become history.

Hash Knife directors ordered a liquidation of the cattle. The older steers were rounded up first and shipped to Kansas. The dry cows were next. Mother cows and their calves were left with what forage remained in the mountains, canyons, and draws until they, too, were gathered for shipment. Surprisingly, they were in good health despite range conditions. Approximately 33,000 cattle were sold for $14 a head.[98] At the close of the 1899 shipping season, the *Holbrook*

Argus reported on the number of cattle moved out of Hash Knife country by rail: "Nearly 20,000 head of cattle has been shipped from Holbrook and vicinity this summer. From Holbrook, 13,000 head, Winslow, 6,000 head and Navajo about 1000 head."[99]

After fourteen years of a turbulent existence, the frontier cattle empire of the Aztec Land and Cattle Company died with the nineteenth century. Reasons given were its losses from wholesale cattle rustling and overstocked ranges, a drop in stock prices brought on by the Spanish-American War, a prolonged drought that started in 1895, and the devastating winter of 1898–99 that killed cattle by the thousands.

On September 29, 1900, the *Holbrook Argus* reported: "Burton Mossman shipped nine cars of cattle last Sunday [September 23] for the Aztec Land and Cattle company. This company has but few cattle left and will soon be out of the business altogether."[100] With that, Mossman ended his connection with the company. Partly as a

Hash Knife chuck wagon in Holbrook, Arizona Territory, in 1901. On the ground is horse wrangler J. C. ("Judge") Lathrop. On the wagon, *left to right,* are Frank Wallace, manager, George W. Hennessey, and Johnny Hoffman. Sitting below Hoffman is Emmett Wallace, son of the Hash Knife manager. (J. & W. Seligman & Co. Archives, Bass Business Collection, University of Oklahoma, Norman)

result of his success in capturing cattle thieves for the Hash Knife, Mossman helped organize the Arizona Rangers early in 1901, at the request of the territorial governor. On August 20 of that year he received a commission as the first captain of the new statewide force of mounted lawmen.[101]

7

Rhyming Robber of
the Hash Knife

ROUND 11 P.M. on May 30, 1888, the A. & B. Schuster General Merchandise store in Holbrook was robbed of $200 in checks. According to the *St. Johns Herald*, Adolf Schuster was in the store alone, his twin brother having retired to his room at the rear of the building. The robber entered with gun drawn and ordered the safe opened. He emptied a cigar box of checks and was leaving when Ben Schuster appeared with a shotgun and fired. The robber was struck by some of the lead from the shotgun blast. Pieces of cloth from his coat were later found embedded in the holes made by the buckshot in the door casing through which he made his exit.[1] He was not disguised, and both merchants recognized him as Red McNeil.[2]

A devil-may-care Hash Knife cowboy, known in Arizona and New Mexico as "Red," W. R. McNeil turned robber in 1887 at age twenty. He became a legend by insulting victims and lawmen alike with taunting rhymes and notes either left at the scene of his crimes or mailed to them or to the press.

Flagstaff historian Platt Cline told a story about this colorful redhead in 1947. He had compiled it from newspaper accounts and stories related by old-timers who knew McNeil. It was commonly believed that he came from a wealthy family, and he was generally considered a "remittance man" who had been educated in a big university back East. Cline also wrote that he was known in Flag-

staff, Winslow, and Holbrook as "a worthless, harum-scarum youngster with an aversion for work and an affinity for barrooms."[3] McNeil once revealed to his friend Bill Lee of Winslow that he had been educated to be a Catholic priest.[4]

Red McNeil was wanted in Arizona and New Mexico for horse stealing. He "broke jail" in Phoenix and helped himself to a horse belonging to another man. Recaptured near Duncan around the middle of January 1888 by a deputy sheriff from Florence, within a week he had escaped from the Florence jail.[5]

Time may not have allowed the desperado to create a lengthy composition about the Schuster robbery by the next morning, but a short poem attributed to McNeil was said to have been found posted on a large tree trunk on the south side of the Little Colorado River.

In it he bragged on his personal feats and ridiculed Sheriff Commodore P. Owens for his ineptness.[6] A longer poetic effusion attributed to him, which contains the same material, was published nearly a year later in a St. Johns newspaper:

I'm the prince of the Aztecs;
I am perfection at robbing a store;
I have a stake left me by Wells Fargo,
And before long I will have more.

On trains I have made a good haul—
Stages are things I hate—
My losses are always small,
My profits exceedingly great.

I will say a few words for my friends,
You see I have quite a few;
And although we are at dagger's ends,
I would like to say, "How d'ye do."

There are McKinney and Larsen,
Who say that robbers have no honor.
I think in a test of manhood,
They'd have to stand back in a corner.

There are my friends, the Schusters,
For whom I carry so much lead;
In the future, to kill this young rooster,
They will have to shoot at his head.

Commodore Owens says he wants to kill me;
To me that sounds like fun.
'Tis strange he'd thus try to kill me,
The red-headed son-of-a-gun.

He handles a six-shooter neat,
And hits a rabbit every pop;
But should he and I happen to meet,
We'll have an old-fashioned Arkansas [hop].

The original A. & B. Schuster general store in Holbrook. Less than a month after it was robbed by Red McNeil, the building burned to the ground in a disastrous fire that swept through the town on June 26, 1888. Adolf Schuster is the third man from the left and Ben Schuster the fifth from the left. (Courtesy of Charles E. Lisitzky)

My friends, I will have to leave you;
  My war horse is sniffing the breeze;
I wish I could stay here to see you—
  Make yourselves at home, if you please.

I will not say very much more,
  My space is growing so small—
You're always welcome to my share.
  What's that? "Much obliged." Not at all. [7]

The posse sent out to hunt McNeil the morning after the robbery returned to Holbrook empty-handed later in the day. On the following morning, June 1, Adolph Schuster swore out a warrant, but McNeil was never arrested for the robbery. [8]

In August 1888, a wanted poster offering a $1,000 reward for McNeil, alias Wallace, alias King, was circulated after he stole a thoroughbred sorrel stallion at or near Alma, New Mexico. [9] The victim of the robbery, William French, who managed the WS spread in southwest New Mexico, later wrote the story.

McNeil rode up to the ranch as a "Chuck-liner," a name given to cowboys out of work who depended on the hospitality of different ranches for "food and fodder." French thought it was strange that McNeil had four fine horses with him that bore the Hash Knife brand. The cowboy explained that when he left the outfit, he asked to receive his pay in horseflesh. The fact that the brands were unvented was, according to him, because he left in a hurry and did not want to scar the animals and thus reduce their value. The redheaded stranger, who identified himself as William McNeil, entertained the WS boys royally with his mouth harp and clog dancing. Everyone at the ranch accepted him.

French and most of his cowboys left for cow camp in a day or so, and McNeil remained behind with a small ranch crew. A few days later, two messengers rode out to the distant camp at breakneck speed with the startling news that the thoroughbred sire, Pow-a-Sheik, had been stolen out of the stable. Gone too was the clog dancer.

William French drew up a proclamation offering a reward of $1,000 for the arrest of William McNeil, alias James Howe, with a description of the robber and the horse. A lawyer in Silver City had several hundred wanted posters printed and sent to all local newspapers in the bordering counties of New Mexico and Arizona. For nearly a month, cowboys from the ranch searched the surrounding country all the way to the Tonto Basin in Arizona, where they found they were in more disfavor than the horse thief.

When he returned to the ranch, French found a stack of letters awaiting him as a result of the reward posters. One was a fat, dirty envelope that had evidently been carried for some time before it was mailed in Clifton, Arizona. He was astonished to find an altered poster inside the envelope, "all done with very different ink, a decrepit pen, and a very primitive hand," naming him the wanted man with the reward being offered by William McNeil, alias James Howe! The humorous gesture made French a little less hostile toward his adversary.[10]

Meanwhile, Sheriff Commodore P. Owens of Apache County, Arizona, was searching for McNeil between Holbrook and the New Mexico line. He rode into one cow camp to inquire whether anyone there knew the wanted man. All disclaimed any knowledge of him.

Owens asked to spend the night, and one of the young cowboys shared his bedroll with the sheriff. The *Arizona Champion* reported on September 22, 1888, that during his stay the lawman never showed any suspicion that his "bed-fellow was the noted horse thief that he was then in quest of."[11]

When Owens awoke the next morning, his hosts were gone. Pinned to his covers was a note stating that his bedfellow was an early riser and could not wait for the sheriff to get up. As an additional affront, the following poem was added:

Pardon me, sheriff
I'm in a hurry;
You'll never catch me
But don't you worry.

The message was signed "Red McNeil."[12]

Back in New Mexico, one of the WS cowboys was still in the saddle looking for the prize stallion. He discovered a single hoofprint on an old Indian trail that led west toward Arizona. It appeared to be about the size that Pow-a-Sheik would make, but it was flat and smooth. The cowboy returned to the ranch but was back the next morning with his boss. Like all Indian paths, this trail was difficult to follow. The two wondered how McNeil ever found the route. They figured the trail would eventually strike the Frisco (San Francisco River) or the Blue, so they made their way to an acquaintance, "Stuttering Bob" Johnson, who had a cabin on Little Blue River in Arizona. Before they reached their destination, the odd-looking hoofprint showed up from time to time. At one place they were forced to follow a trail, almost impassable in spots, over a long side hill that contained a shelving rock of forty to fifty yards in length. They again found the track of the horse at the edge of the rock where the dirt had been stirred up by the stamp and shuffle of hoofs. The rock itself bore scars where the horse had slid. William French described the rough trail that still lay ahead for him and his cowboy:

Shortly after reaching the bottom we got into the narrowest canyon it has ever been my lot to enter. It looked like a tunnel, and though it extended for some two or three miles there was no single

place in which two horsemen could ride abreast. For almost the en-
tire distance you could spread out your arms and touch the roof on
either side. We sincerely hoped that it would not rain while we were
in there, for the drift-wood was jammed across the canyon from
seventy-five to a hundred feet over our heads. The top must have
been fully a thousand feet up, for although it was not very late in
the afternoon the stars were distinctly visible.[13]

The two trackers reached Johnson's cabin around sunset. After they explained their mission, their host declared that they must be following a man who called himself the "Red-headed Rooster." From an obscure corner of the room he produced a saddle, bridle, and blankets he had bought from the same man, whose horse had been killed and left him afoot. The two guests immediately recognized the gear as having belonged to McNeil.

The story told by Stuttering Bob cleared up the peculiar tracks followed by the boss of the WS and his cowhand. McNeil had told Johnson that his horse had become sore-footed and had thrown his shoes. The rider killed a calf and shod all four feet with the fresh hide, which made round, flat impressions. When they reached a shelving rock on the trail, the mount became frightened and McNeil tried to lead him. The horse reared up and fell backward over a drop of about one hundred feet, rolled seven or eight hundred feet more, and stopped at a clump of brush at the bottom, below the same spot on the trail where the two trackers had had difficulty the day before. On the following day, their host showed French the carcass of Pow-a-Sheik at the bottom of the canyon below the treacherous rock shelf.[14]

In early 1889, Pete Jacoby of Winslow made an extensive hunt for McNeil's Arizona hideout. In April he located it in Clear Creek Canyon, forty miles south of Winslow. When he returned to town, he proposed to local authorities that a purse and posse be raised to capture McNeil. Within twenty-four hours, the citizens of Winslow raised $1,000 and a posse of three men, including Sheriff John Francis of Coconino County.

The armed group arrived in late afternoon in the vicinity of the McNeil stronghold, located in the deep, narrow, and precipitous canyon, approachable only from two directions. Instead of dividing and advancing from both ends, the whole posse moved from the east toward the hideout. As they neared the cabin, one of the men happened to look across the creek to the opposite side of the canyon. There stood McNeil, high up among the rocks, watching their every movement with rifle in hand.

When the firing commenced, McNeil jumped behind a large boulder. The battle lasted for over a hour. Realizing that their initial strategy had failed, the posse decided to make a flanking movement, working its way to the head of the canyon and approaching the hideout from the west side. The detour consumed so much time that McNeil was gone by the time members of the posse got there. They did find a note in the cabin in which he expressed his regrets at having to leave and condemned those who took part in the nearby Canyon Diablo train robbery, which had occurred only a month before and caused a sensation. He added a postscript stating that the posse owed him some ammunition.

> *Dear Friends—I hope you will not be insulted at the reception I gave you, for you see that it was my birthday, and I thought I would celebrate it with a pyrotechnical exhibition on a small scale. I have so few visitors here, that I am glad to have some one come around, no matter what his business is, I am always ready to welcome him by firing a few shots from my Winchester as a salute. Some people do not admire this style of greeting—but they cannot see a joke. I hope you, my cunning friends, will appreciate it at its full value. People say the train has been robbed. This is terrible. Who robbed it? I do hope and trust that you, gentlemen, will do all in your power to capture the guilty parties. Run them to their rendezvous; give them no quarter. Such depredations should be stopped at once. With best wishes, I remain yours, til Clear Creek runs dry.*
>
> *P.S.—You, gentlemen, owe me a box of 44-calibre cartridges.*[15]

A month after the gunfight, the self-styled "prince of the Aztecs" appeared to be leaving Arizona. On May 16, 1889, it was reported in the newspaper that he had been seen in Holbrook "a few days since" where he mailed another poem to the press, took a horse from a local stable, and casually rode off. When he stopped for a short visit with a friend, he was said to be riding a brown horse and leading a sorrel

stallion as a pack animal. Apparently unconcerned about being arrested, the daring McNeil employed a Navajo to pilot him across the
reservation in a northerly direction. By now, a lenient press was
yielding politely to the affable bandit: "There is something to ad-
mire in such dare-devil recklessness, when it is known he has never
shed the blood of his fellowman."[16]

A poetic reminder of the most recent hostilities was said to have
been sent through the mail to Sheriff John Francis of Coconino
County:

> *Here's where Clear Creek deeply flows,*
> *From the melted mass of Mogollon snows;*
> *Here I lived and fain would roam*
> *O'er the country that I, for years, called home.*
> *Hunted continually, like some wild beast,*
> *Until I reached my ranch I knew no peace.*
> *While strolling on the canyon side,*
> *Three men on the opposite side I spied.*
> *They were officers—bold, brave men.*
> *Who dared to brave the lion in his den.*
> *They little dreamed of the danger near*
> *Until a report, which startled all,*
> *Quickly followed by a whistling ball.*
> *Nothing could excel the leader's grace*
> *As he threw his rifle to his face,*
> *And as my carbine rang out, crack,*
> *He quickly sent an answer back.*
> *In fighting, these officers were well-skilled,*
> *Yet strange to say, none were killed.*
> *But among the pines birds whispered that*
> *A bullet pierced Jacob[y]'s hat;*
> *And as the battle held its course,*
> *Another struck John Francis' horse.*
> *Although my name is badly smudged*
> *Toward these men I hold no grudge,*
> *And hope some day a free man to stand*
> *And grasp my combatants by the hand.*[17]

Around June 26, Red McNeil, using the name Edward K. Dayton, arrived at Sage Hen Flat, about five miles below the Big Bend of the Delores River in southwest Colorado. There he made the acquaintance of an eighteen-year-old farm youth named Joseph B. Nay and spent two weeks at the home of the boy's parents. During his stay, the young men made plans to rob a train of the Denver & Rio Grande Western Railroad.

Telling his parents he was going to a nearby town to work, Joseph assumed the name Joe Dayton and left with his companion, now identified as his older brother. They went south into New Mexico where they changed horses and then headed north to the Blue Mountains in the Monticello area of southeast Utah. After spending about three weeks there, the two began the last lap of their journey north, riding at night and resting during the day. Three days later, they reached Thompson Springs and the railroad line. Near Moab they day before, the couple had made face masks to wear during the robbery.

The experienced highwayman and his apprentice stayed at Thompson Springs two days to allow their horses to rest. On August 6, 1889, they tied the mounts about three miles from the depot, where they could not be seen from the tracks, and walked back to the station. Half an hour later, as the train slowed up by the water tank, the two men donned their masks and got on behind the tender. Both had Colt .45's, with one .44 Winchester between them. When the locomotive reached the area where the horses were left, the robbers ordered the engineer to stop the train. Joe guarded the engineer and fireman while Red made his way to the express car. He rapped on the door with his six-shooter and demanded that it be opened. Failing to get a response from the messenger, he tried but failed to break down the door with an ax. In his frustration, he emptied twenty-five rounds of ammunition into the door of the car but to no effect. He then made the engineer carry a sack alongside him through the cars while he forced the passengers to empty their pockets and purses of all valuables.

The outlaws then mounted their horses and headed south for the Blue Mountains. At Courthouse Rocks, twenty-seven miles south of the scene of the robbery, they stopped and counted the money taken. The greenbacks, gold, and silver totaled $125. Five watches were in the loot. They divided the money, sold one watch, and threw the other four away. The pair then rode to Montrose, Colorado, where they sold their horses and the rifle used in the robbery. They left Montrose later in the month and on September 1 reached Ogden, Utah.[18]

A week later, an employee of Maden's saloon in Ogden was robbed of $336 at gunpoint at 1:40 in the morning by an unidentified man. The worker was carrying a sack of silver down the stairway from the gambling hall through the crowded saloon to the company safe when the holdup occurred. As the robber made good his escape down the darkened street, he shot a local citizen in the leg.[19]

Ten days later, a man who called himself Edward Dayton was arrested for the robbery. He was stripped of his coat and vest, and the officers found on his person a Commercial National Bank sack that contained twenty-two silver dollars. He also had two pocketbooks and a few trinkets on him. One newspaper reporter wrote about a treasured possession that was uppermost in the mind of the robber: "A mouth organ which he particularly asked for must not be forgotten among the effects." Later that afternoon, a man believed to be an accomplice was arrested at the depot. He stated that his name was J. E. Dayton, born in Circle Valley on the Sevier River in Utah, and that he was a brother of the man previously taken into custody. He claimed to know nothing about the saloon robbery, but authorities were sure they now had the two men who had pulled off the D & RG train robbery.[20]

A visitor in town from Cortez, Colorado, had seen the train robbers just after the crime was committed and knew all the particulars. He recognized the two on the streets of Ogden and had alerted lawmen earlier that they were in town.[21] Faced with this evidence and that of a detective who was placed in a cell next to them and overheard their conversations about the holdup, the prisoners confessed to their crimes.[22] At this time, the elder said that his name was E. K. Fisher.

Another newspaper reporter was able to get some details about Fisher's early life. According to the prisoner, he was born in a suburb of Boston in April 1867. His father and mother had both died by the time he was five years old. He then went to live with relatives until he was fourteen, when he went to Texas and became engaged in ranching and handling stock.[23]

On September 25, a true bill of indictment was returned against Ed Fisher and Joseph Nay for the robbery of the passenger train near Thompson Springs. They waived examinations and were transferred to the Utah Penitentiary at Sugar House. E. K. Fisher, alias B. W. McNeil, alias Ed Dayton, entered prison on September 26, 1889. The occupation of the twenty-two-year-old Massachusetts native was listed as cowboy. He was described as being five feet ten inches tall and weighing 170 pounds. For his Utah crimes, Fisher received two consecutive sentences of seven years for train robbery, two years for assault with a deadly weapon, and eight years for robbery. Joseph Nay was imprisoned on the same day as Fisher under a sentence of five and a half years for train robbery.

When the penitentiary registration of Fisher was transferred to the record books of the Utah State Prison, following statehood in 1896, an entry was made of an additional alias, Wallace McNeil. Wallace was one of many surnames used by the robber in Arizona. After serving nearly ten years, the older prisoner, known in Arizona as Red McNeil, was released from prison on June 3, 1899. Joseph Nay had been discharged on April 26, 1893.[24]

In the 1920s, the former Hash Knife cowboy displayed some remorse about his wild Arizona past when he wrote to a Navajo County friend and asked if the Schusters "were still mad at him." He was assured by return mail that the incident was practically forgotten. Some time later, a dignified and professional-looking man appeared at the Schuster store in Holbrook to see Ben Schuster. When told Ben had died, he asked for Adolf Schuster. McNeil introduced himself to the proprietor as a former resident of Holbrook. They talked about the old days, but the visitor never revealed his identity.[25]

In 1928, Red McNeil again called on Adolf Schuster, who was living at that time in Los Angeles, California.[26] He told the surviving Schuster brother who he was and said that he had educated himself to be a hydraulic engineer while serving time in the Utah penitentiary. A daughter of Schuster later recalled that the former

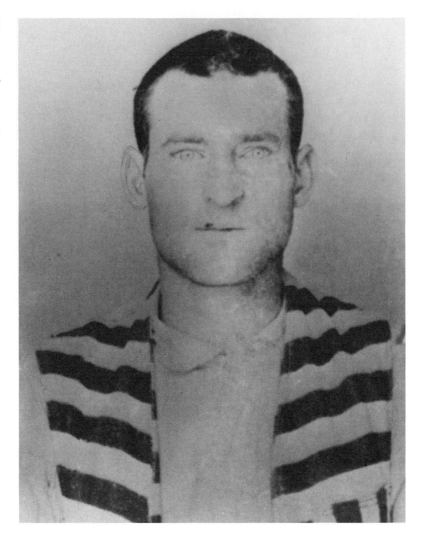

Utah Penitentiary mug shot, taken in 1889, of E. K. Fisher, known in Arizona as Red McNeil, the rhyming robber of the Hash Knife. (Utah State Prison)

adversaries had a good time swapping yarns. Her only regret was that the stranger was gone before she learned about the brief encounter between him and her father forty years earlier.[27]

Only the year before, William French had published his memoirs as a ranchman in New Mexico. He had heard of the imprisonment of McNeil in Utah but nothing after that. Yet, despite the loss of his great stallion Pow-a-Sheik, he apparently held some fond memories of the rhyming robber of the Hash Knife: "I never heard what became of him—whether he died in prison or served his time out. If the latter, I bet he came out playing his mouth-harp and danced a double shuffle on the pavement."[28]

8

Songs on the Hash
Knife Range

THE acknowledged troubadour of the old Hash Knife outfit in Arizona was Fall-Back Joe. Will Barnes said Joe might have had a last name, but in five years on the range he had never heard him called by it. The Hash Knife wrangler, whose voice scattered on him at times, had a left leg six inches shorter than the right, which made him walk with an odd gait and earned him the name Fall-Back Joe. His horse had to be "Injun broke" so it could be mounted from the right side.[1]

Fall-Back Joe's favorite song by far was "Lorena." Frequently, he sat around the campfire in the evening and sang about the lonely girl who waited at home for a lover who never returned. Every man in camp knew the song, and it was sung so often day and night that the cranky Hash Knife cook, Rickety Bob, threatened to take his pothook and beat up anyone who even hummed it around the wagon.

The last shipment of Hash Knife cattle for the season was a cause for celebration. At the height of the revelry, company cowboys would boost Fall-Back Joe up on the long bar in the Bucket of Blood Saloon and request "Lorena." A few supportive singers would help Joe lengthen the song by repeating the last two lines of each verse as a refrain. Hardened cowboys did nothing to hide their tears during the renditions, but their sentimentality had better not be mentioned the next day.

Probably because of poor memory on the part of the singers,

Barnes printed only four incomplete verses to the sentimental favorite of the Hash Knife cowboys:

Lorena

Oh, the years creep slowly by, Lorena
 The snow is on the grass again.
The sun's low down the sky, Lorena.
 The frost gleams where the [flow'rs] have been.

A hundred months have passed, Lorena,
 Since last I held that hand in mine,
And felt that pulse beat fast, Lorena,
 Though mine beat faster far than thine.

We loved each other then, Lorena,
 More than we ever dared to tell,
Oh, what we might have been, Lorena,
 Had but our lovings prospered well.

It matters little now, Lorena;
 The past is in the eternal past.
Our heads will soon lie low, Lorena;
 Life's tide is ebbing out so fast.[2]

Rickety Bob allowed sarcastically that "a hundred months, meanin' nigh onto eight and a third years, was a powerful long time to re-co-lect a gal's pulse" like the song said.[3]

"Lorena" was written in 1857 by Universalist clergyman Henry De Lafayette Webster and New Hampshire composer Joseph Philbrick Webster.[4] Although they shared the same surname, they were not related. The song was a particular favorite with Confederate soldiers, and the endearing Lorena became their mythical sweetheart.[5] No doubt the song was carried to the cattle country by former soldiers, as was another favorite song among Hash Knife cowboys, "Tenting on the Old Camp Ground," written in 1863 by Walter Kittredge, another New Hampshire composer as well as an itinerant singer of note.

A former co-worker was responsible for the unusual name of the Holbrook establishment—the Bucket of Blood—where the Hash Knife cowboys did their drinking and harmonizing. During the spring roundup of 1887, two riders approached the camp of Albert F. Potter at a lake twelve miles east of Holbrook where a herd of Potter's was being held. They rode up at sunrise from the direction of town. They were thought at first to be Indians because one had a cloth wrapped Indian fashion around his head, but he proved to be Joe Crawford, who had worked for the Hash Knife at one time. The other was George Bell, a gambler. Crawford was seriously wounded from a blow to the head and had lost a lot of blood. With a handful of flour from the chuck wagon box, Potter plastered the head of the cowboy to stop the bleeding. A bullet had passed through a coat sleeve and grazed the side of his body. Potter noticed that Crawford also had scars on his body from old gunshot wounds.

George Bell told the cow crew that he and Crawford had been in a card game with Ramon Lopez and another Mexican in a saloon known as the Cottage. A disagreement arose, and Lopez bashed Crawford over the head with a six-shooter. Crawford drew his gun and killed his assailant. When the other Mexican reached for his gun, Crawford fired again and down went his second victim.

Around the middle of the day, Hash Knife cowboy Tom South rode into camp with the news that no warrant had been issued for the two. The roundup boss saw no reason to detain the visitors and told them they were free to go. The report by South proved to be false, but by the time a lawman arrived in camp Crawford and Bell were gone.

In the Holbrook barroom where the two Mexicans had sprawled in death, there remained a spot on the floor that looked as if a bucket of blood had been spilled there. Following the disastrous fire in Holbrook in 1888, the Cottage was renamed the Bucket of Blood. The general belief in Holbrook at that time was that Crawford was in fact Grat Dalton, a member of the notorious family gang of Kansas outlaws, on one of his trips between home and California.[6]

Other popular songs on the early Hash Knife ranges were picked up at saloons, barbershops, and cheap shows and from other cowboys. According to Will Barnes, the new singers adapted the songs to their own environment simply by changing some of the words. In addition to "Lorena" and "Tenting on the Old Camp Ground," the repertory of the ranch crew included "Belle Mahone," "Juanita," "Old Folks at Home," "Annie Laurie," "Darling Nelly Gray," and the 1864 temperance song of Henry Clay Work, "Come Home, Father."

One Hash Knife cowboy, known as the Hoosier Kid, sang the only song he knew, "I'm a Pilgrim," night after night as he circled the herd: "within a country, unknown and dreary, / I have been wandering, forlorn and weary."

"Sam Bass," a song about a cowboy who went bad, was popular not only on Hash Knife ranges but all over the West. Wandering minstrels of the gentler sex attracted customers in drinking places by singing in a semihumorus strain "The Cowgirl's Lament" and one of the bawdiest of all cowboy ballads, "The Bucking Broncho."

"The Cowboy's Sweet By-and-By" is a product of the cowboy, with the title suggested by the 1868 gospel song "Sweet By and By" and the tune from the traditional Scottish song "My Bonnie Lies Over the Ocean." Will Barnes heard the cowboy hymn sung for the first time on the Hash Knife ranges in 1886 or 1887 by a halfbreed Indian from southern Utah. He added verses of his own and later sang the song, along with "The Zebra Dun" and "Across the Big Divide," during a successful campaign for the Arizona legislature.

Popular with native Texans in northern Arizona were "The Dying Ranger" and "The Lone Prairie." A favorite all over the cattle country, "The Cowboy's Lament," was sung around the Hash Knife camps by a youngster called the Texas Kid.

One of the most celebrated of all early range songs was "My Lulu Gal," containing hundreds of verses made up by cowboys to suit any environment or situation in which they found themselves. The song told of the amours, flirtations, and general cussedness of Lulu, but only a few verses could be sung in polite society.[7]

One ballad of local origin sung by Fall-Back Joe was about Mose Tate, who worked for a number of cattle outfits in Arizona, including the Hash Knife. Moses Robert Tate was born on April 4, 1836, in Montgomery County, Kentucky.[8] He became a cowman early in life and accumulated a small fortune in Texas before an extended drought and disease among his livestock wiped him out. He then began life anew as a cowboy.[9] In 1875 Tate was working for cattle baron Charles Goodnight and helped drive the first cattle herd that ever entered the Texas Panhandle.

In the spring of 1875, Goodnight placed his brother-in-law, Leigh

Dyer, in charge of one of his cattle herds in Colorado and instructed
him to drift eastward along the Arkansas River and locate on Two
Butte Creek south of Las Animas. Goodnight rejoined the outfit in
the fall and pointed his herd of 1,600 head south toward the Staked
Plains (Llano Estacado), crossing the Cimarron, then to the south
bank of the Canadian River in eastern New Mexico. They went into
winter camp on Rano Creek and another small stream ten miles
west.[10]

The following summer, the Goodnight herd entered the Texas
Panhandle and made its way southeast by way of "the old Comanche
Trail" to the caprock of Palo Duro Canyon. In late November,
buffalo were driven out the mouth of the canyon to the east while the
cattle were slowly moved down a rugged, narrow trail to the upper

end of the canyon floor, where Charles Goodnight established the first ranch in the Texas Panhandle.[11] Others beside Mose Tate who took part in the historic drive included J. T. Hughes, J. C. Johnston, Jim Owens, Dave McCormick, and Argie Argo.[12]

When the LE Ranch was founded in Oldham and Hartley counties in 1879 by W. M. D. Lee and A. E. Reynolds, Mose Tate was named manager on a favorable endorsement from Charles Goodnight. It was said that Tate "managed more men with fewer words than any other man in all the Panhandle." Tate and LE cowboy Bob Elkins left ranch headquarters early one morning to do a job on a distant part of the range. Mose had not been feeling well. As they were leaving, Elkins asked the foreman how he felt but got no response. Neither spoke for the rest of the day. As they approached the ranch house late that evening, Mose answered, "I believe I feel better today."[13]

In February 1882, Mose Tate arrived in northern Arizona. Three years later, the St. Johns newspaper commented on the esteem in which he was held: "Moses Tate, one of Apache counties most respected settlers, paid the county seat one of his semi-occasional visits on Sunday."[14]

Tate worked at various times for the Waters Cattle Company, whose range included Clear Creek and Chevelon Fork of the Little Colorado River. He became the company foreman in early April 1887 when the manager of the ranch was replaced.[15] By midsummer, however, Mose was working for a new cattle outfit.

Two years earlier, Glenn Reynolds of the Reynolds Land and Cattle Company in Shackelford County, Texas, had helped drive a herd of cattle to northern Arizona for Jess Ellison, a neighboring rancher. A small part of the herd belonged to Reynolds himself. In 1886 he went back to Texas and returned with another herd that belonged to his brothers.[16] A large number of the cattle were branded with the well-known Spur brand from Texas.[17]

On August 27, 1887, the *Apache County Critic* reported that the Reynolds herd in Arizona had been sold to the Defiance Cattle Company. It also announced that Mose Tate would "receive and take charge" of more than 1,000 head of stock for the firm.[18] (When

Mose Tate, on the tall horse in the center of the photograph, is flanked by Hash Knife cowboys at the Old Aztec Land and Cattle Company headquarters in 1888. (National Archives, Washington, D.C.)

Gila County was organized, Reynolds was elected its first sheriff. He was killed by the Apache Kid on November 2, 1889.)

J. H. Bowman, representing the Defiance Cattle Company, a New York corporation, recorded the Spur brand on June 25, 1888, in Apache County.[19] Company cattle were run on railroad land in the Tanner Springs country northwest of Navajo, Arizona. A high-spirited song with numerous situation couplets, called "The Dad-Blamed Boss," soon evolved about "Old Mose Tate, the old Spur boss." A cowboy who made up at least the second verse identified himself as Dick.

Will Barnes, whose spread joined the Hash Knife, preserved the words to the song about Mose. Its tune and frivolous refrain were both borrowed from "Up the Old Chisholm Trail." Barnes wrote a musical arrangement of its antecedent, which he also collected in Arizona.

Arthur Chapman, a contemporary of Barnes, was well-known for his popular poem "Out Where the West Begins," which later became a song itself. Chapman supplied Barnes with a couplet to the Mose Tate song, printed here as the fourth verse. Chapman had heard the song under the title "Mose Tate."[20]

The Dad-Blamed Boss

1. *Oh, here I am a-settin' on my hoss,*
   An' spoonin' these old cows fer that dad-blamed boss.

Cho. *Come-a-tie-wy-waddy, inkie-eye-eye-a-a-a.*
   Come-a-tie-wy-waddy-inkie-eye.

Come a runnin' all you cowboys
  Come an' lissen to my tale.
An' I'll tell you all a story
  Of the old Chisholm trail.
    Come a tie-wy-waddy
      Inkie eye-eye aye.
    Come a tie wy waddy
      inkie aye.

Oh we rounded up the cattle
  Then we cut out all tho bulls
    An' we branded all the dogies
    An' throwed 'em with the culls.
      Come a tie-wy-waddy
        etc.

I dumped my roll of beddin'
  Near the old chuck wagons tail
For the outfit was a headin'
  Up the old Chisholm trail.
    Come a tie-wy-waddy etc

The song about Mose Tate was sung to the tune of this Arizona variant of the well-known cowboy ballad "The Old Chisholm Trail." (Barnes Collection, Box 13, Folder 91, n.d., Arizona Historical Society Library, Tucson)

2. *Oh, the boss he says, "Dick, kin ye ride a pitchin' hoss?"*
    "I kin ride 'em in the slick," I tells that dad-blamed boss.

3. *Now there's Old Mose Tate, the old Spur boss.*
    He'd rather ride a navvy than a hundred-dollar hoss.

4. *He kin ride a sore-toed hoss with a quirt in his hand,*
    An' can cut more old cows than any damned man.

5. *Oh, the boss says, "Mose, don't you get on your ear,*
    An' I'll buy some good hosses to ride next year."

6. *We rounded up the cattle an' cut out all the steers;*
    We branded all the calves an' put the Spur mark in their
    ears.

7. *I'll get me a new slicker an' some Coffeyville boots,*
    Buy a quart of good red licker an' quit this crazy old galoot.

8. *Oh, I'll shake this job tomorrow, pack my soogins on a hoss*
    An' pull my freight fer Texas, where there ain't no dad-
    blamed boss.

No doubt the song about Mose Tate was sung in jest, because he had "an excellent name in range circles of the north, and was of a very generous nature."[21] One verse jokingly states that he preferred to ride a Navajo pony that would have been worth about ten dollars.

Barnes wrote about the relationship of the Mose Tate song to his variant of the Chisholm Trail ballad: "Growling about the boss or bawling out the outfit you worked for was a favorite sport with cowboys, and formed the basis of yards and yards of alleged poetry that invariably had the same chorus and was sung to the same nasal, jerky little old tune no matter where the artist came from."[22]

The singers, and the writer of one couplet, were serious about their choice of boots, the prized, bench-made Coffeyville footwear made by John W. Cubine in his small shop in Coffeyville, Kansas. The market price for Cubine boots ran from six to twelve dollars a pair up to eighteen or twenty dollars, depending upon how many tramp shoemakers drifted into town and how long they stayed. The price also varied according to how many stars, crescents, horse-shoes, or "bleeding hearts" were embroidered on the fancy-stitched

legs.[23] Another distinction of the Coffeyville boot was that it was one of the first products of its kind to feature a right and left boot rather than an identical pair that were interchangeable until they shaped themselves from constant wear.[24] One northern Arizona cowboy commented about the Cubine boots: "Next to our saddles, a pair of Coffeyville boots was the choicest thing in this life, something every rider coveted and bought if it took his last cent."[25] A nephew of the famous cobbler and a bootmaker himself, George Cubine was killed during the infamous street battle with the Dalton gang in 1892, along with three other Coffeyville citizens.

Mose Tate went to Apache County as a range rider for the Aztec Land and Cattle Company and reached the grade of foreman. Although known primarily in Arizona as a Hash Knife cowboy, he did work for various other cattle outfits off and on for short periods of time. On May 12, 1900, the *Holbrook Argus* reported that Mose was in town from Aztec headquarters and added, "Mr. Tate is probably one of the oldest cowmen in this section, having been on the frontier for many years, being over 60 years of age."[26]

Mose Tate was admitted to the Arizona Pioneers' Home in Prescott on April 4, 1911. Because the aged cowboy had no known relatives, Hash Knife officials Frank Wallace of Adamana and Captain Henry M. Warren of St. Joseph were listed as contact persons to handle his private affairs. While in the rest home, the legendary Mose died on October 8, 1918, "from intestinal problems."[27]

9

Trouble between Cowboys and Navajos

BAD feelings had existed for years between cowboys and Navajos along the Little Colorado. Both sides were probably at fault. Whether intentionally or not, the big cattle outfits were usurping the ranges of the Navajos, who in return were straying off the reservation to hunt game and to take horses that may not have belonged to them.

The Little Colorado River was considered the boundary between the Navajo Reservation to the north and the vast ranges of the cattle outfits to the south. Cattlemen also controlled the west side of the river after it made its turn due north at Winslow.

The majority of Hash Knife cattle came from Texas to Arizona by rail. When trail herds passed through, however, some of the country in between was so well stocked with resident cattle that trouble erupted between owners. According to one cattleman already in business in northern Arizona, almost 40,000 hungry cows, calves, steers, and bulls of the Aztec Land and Cattle Company were unloaded at the railroad yards and allowed to "drift yonderly."[1] At every spring roundup, it was found that some of the immigrant bovines had strayed over into the breaks of the Painted Desert north of the river, unoccupied except for scattered Navajo herders and their sheep. Other companies were having the same trouble.

During the 1887 spring roundup of the Reynolds Cattle Company east of Holbrook, eight or ten cowboys attempted to retrieve some of their strays that had worked their way over into Navajo country. The men were surrounded by a large group of angry Navajos and, under threat of death, were forced to leave empty-handed.[2]

By the spring of 1894, the consensus among cattlemen was that a general roundup of all their cattle north and east of the Little Colorado was the only way to gather strays that by now had reverted to the wild. For five weeks the roundup crew worked the Navajo country for cattle, gathering about 800 head. When they returned to Winslow, they were told the cattle could not be shipped because of a railroad strike that had occurred during their absence. The only recourse for the cowboys was to drive the unruly herd south to the Mogollon Rim and "cut out" bunches every few miles in hopes they would mix with the local cattle and stay there.[3]

Bgwo'ettin ("Teeth Gone") was known to his people as a *hosteen*, a Navajo title that denotes respect. To the cowboys in northern Arizona, he was the headman of a band of renegade Navajos who would not stay inside the reservation. He simply refused to believe that he was a trespasser on ranges that had belonged to his people for generations.

During the Navajo exile from 1863 to 1868, when members of the tribe were rounded up by troops of the First New Mexico Volunteers under Colonel Kit Carson, a youthful Bgwo'ettin made the long walk to the Bosque Redondo on the Pecos River in New Mexico. Back in his homeland after "the Captivity," Bgwo'ettin settled on William D. (Bill) Roden as his main adversary. Roden had begun ranching with his father in 1884 west of the Little Colorado River above Winslow. Bgwo'ettin knew the cowman only as *pezhin'bekhis* ("leatherpants"), the Navajo name for all cowboys.[4]

On Monday, July 13, 1891, Bgwo'ettin was taken into custody outside the reservation near Canyon Diablo on a warrant charging him with horse stealing. The sudden arrest alarmed his followers, and they trailed Sheriff John Francis of Coconino County and nineteen special deputies to their camp. During the night, Francis made his way to the Canyon Diablo station with his prisoner and wired for help. Armed citizens and members of Company C and Company I of the First Regiment N.G.A., forty strong, arrived on Wednesday and rescued the posse.[5]

Three days after his arrest, Bgwo'ettin appeared before Justice

Bgwo'ettin, legendary Navajo headman. (Gladwell Richardson Collection, courtesy of Philip Johnston)

Nelson G. Layton, who ordered his release due to insufficient evidence. Bill Roden immediately swore out a complaint against the Navajo leader for threatening his life. Bgwo'ettin was promptly rearrested and placed under a $2,000 peace bond. D. M. Riordan, Flagstaff merchant and a former government agent on the reservation, hired an attorney to represent Bgwo'ettin, who was found innocent of all charges.[6] Local feelings about the Navajo situation were summed up in the Flagstaff paper: "The trouble between the

Navajos and the settlers along the reservation will always continue until the Government confines them to the limits of their reservation."[7]

The hogans of Bgwo'ettin and his flocks of sheep outside the reservation caused little trouble until cattlemen and their herds moved in. A son of Bgwo'ettin drove his sheep to an ancestral water hole one summer evening as a large herd of cattle driven by two cowboys approached. The sheep were driven away by the intruders, who gave every appearance of establishing a permanent camp and closing the watering place to Navajo sheep. According to Navajo tradition, Indian children would slip over to the spring and fill their casks with water whenever the cowboys were away. They started

William D. (Bill) Roden, early rancher near Grand Falls on the Little Colorado River. (Courtesy of Maryellen Roden)

calling the spring *toh'ba'ja'chin'l* ("stingy water"). Tragedy occurred when tin cans, discarded by cowboys, were used as drinking cups by Navajo children. The Navajo stories, depending upon the version, say that one child died of poisoning, or three children, or a family of seven. The Navajo headman was firm in his belief that the poisoning was deliberate.

General unrest in the area was heightened by a series of unrelated events. At Canyon Diablo, a Navajo woman was killed in 1898, and the Flagstaff militia, formed as a result of the Spanish-American War, apprehended the murderer. Early in 1899, the Flagstaff Blues, as they were called, put down a Navajo uprising without bloodshed near the Canyon Diablo station. Not long after, the busy force captured a band of stock thieves a few miles farther up the gorge.[8]

Mounting tensions between Bgwo'ettin and area cowboys culminated on November 11, 1899, on Hash Knife property, at Padre Canyon, a spur of Canyon Diablo, in what the Flagstaff newspaper emotionally characterized as "one of the most desperate conflicts ever fought in the Southwest." Five days before the fight, a party of Navajos assaulted William A. Montgomery, a young cowboy in the employ of Bill Roden. After abusing him and accusing him of stealing four of their horses, they let him go. Montgomery made his way to Flagstaff and obtained a warrant for the arrest of "John Doe, and Richard Roe, Navajoes."[9]

A Pennsylvania native, Montgomery was known to Bill Roden as William Henry Montgomery and first worked for the rancher in his Wilson Canyon cow camp when the four Hash Knife cowboys held up the train at Canyon Diablo in early 1889. He seemed to know all about the robbery. A few days before the holdup, two of the robbers visited Montgomery in camp and rode out to work with him for three days. The day after the robbery, the young cowboy drew his pay and left, but in 1897 he returned to his old job with Roden. In Phoenix, William Montgomery's father had received a letter written just before the fatal incident with the Navajos in which the young cowboy said he intended to quit the range and return home on the first of December.[10]

On the day of the deadly encounter, Deputy Sheriff Dan Hogan and Special Deputy Walter W. Durham, one of the first Hash Knife cowboys in Arizona, accompanied by Montgomery and Roden,

Hash Knife cowboy Walter W. Durham in 1891. Copy of photograph given to his girlfriend, Deta Neill of Beaver Creek, Arizona Territory, the year before their marriage. (Courtesy of Clarence W. Durham)

made their way to the scene of the assault on the cowboy. When they neared the site, the party picked up Navajo tracks that led to the rim of Anderson Mesa near the head of Padre Canyon, three miles east of Ashurst Spring. They easily located what Deputy Hogan called a "ho-gand," erected by the Navajos at the watering place.[11]

The posse rode into the hostile camp, occupied by seven Navajos, and dismounted. They ground-reined their horses, or "tied" them to the ground, by simply throwing the reins over the ears of the animals and letting the straps trail to the ground. They left their Winchesters on the saddles. One Navajo attempted to get his rifle inside a brush fence that encircled the shelter when Deputy Hogan approached to serve the warrant. A struggle took place between the two, and a shot was fired at Hogan by another Navajo.

At the sound of gunfire, the posse's horses bolted and ran, leaving the lawmen with limited ammunition and handguns only. Montgomery went down with a bullet through his heart when the volley started. Hogan received two flesh wounds, and Roden was hit in the groin. Durham went unscathed. A bullet from his six-gun struck Bgwo'ettin and probably saved Hogan's life. Durham, a former Hash Knife cowboy, later recalled, "I remember watching Dan, who was on his back and struggling with the chief. He was shooting and the chief attempting to, when I stopped him."[12] In addition to Bgwo'ettin's own critically disabling wounds, a son of his was fatally wounded and another Navajo killed instantly. The others escaped into the brush.[13]

Superintendent Burt Mossman of the Aztec Land and Cattle Company and Navajo County Sheriff Frank Wattron were on a late fall hunt in 1899 when the conflict occurred. They were camped at Wild Cat Canyon eighty miles from the scene of the conflict and were unaware of it until they returned to Holbrook.[14]

In a letter to the Commissioner of Indian Affairs in Washington, D.C., dated December 5, 1899, Navajo Agent G. W. Hayzlett told the Indian version of the fight in which "the assaultees on the Indians' side" were two dead and two wounded. According to Navajo participants, they were in their hunting camp when the posse arrived. One of the Navajos sat cleaning his gun. A lawman picked up a deer hide and began asking questions. Bgwo'ettin countered, "Are these your stock?"

At that, the lawmen moved for the Navajos' stacked guns and grabbed two rifles. Bgwo'ettin fought for one and his son for the other. The Navajo who had his gun in hand when the struggle began straightened up and was shot in the stomach. He and two other Navajos, one wounded in the arm and back, ran off. Two others followed. Bgwo'ettin was motionless on the ground with a bullet through his body. A nephew was killed on the spot. His son, mortally wounded in the stomach, fired and hit one of the lawmen who had been shooting at Bgwo'ettin. He then turned and shot another posse member who was firing into the camp. This one fell dead. When the shooting stopped, the officers left the scene on foot.

"The next day," wrote the Navajo agent in his letter, "the old man

Frank Wattron, sheriff of Navajo County (*left*), and Burt Mossman on a hunting trip in Wild Cat Canyon forty miles south of Holbrook, Arizona Territory, in late fall 1899. (Courtesy of Margaret Riseley Barbour)

[Bgwo'ettin] buried his son and left the other where he lay for the reason that it is a belief of theirs that if an Indian is killed by a white man and dies on the spot he should not be touched. The old man's son was buried [because] he moved about after being shot before he died."[15] Wounded in the right leg, rancher Bill Roden had blood spilling out of the top of his boot by the time he and other members of the posse had walked north to the railroad tracks at Winona where they caught a train to Flagstaff.

Bgwo'ettin was carried back to the fastness of the Painted Desert on a blanket slung between two horses. Reverend William R. Johnston, a missionary at Tolchaco on the west side of the Little Colorado, was en route from Oraibi to Flagstaff on horseback. He stopped at the hogan of the Navajo headman where an estimated 1,000 Navajos were gathered, awaiting an attack they believed imminent by soldiers and retaliating whites. Johnston hurried to Flagstaff where Sheriff J. A. Johnson was assembling a large contingent of armed men. The religious leader talked the sheriff into holding his forces in abeyance long enough for Johnston to return alone to the Navajos to appeal to those who were involved in the fight to surrender voluntarily.

Following a long powwow between Johnston and the Navajos, an agreement was reached that two of the battle participants would surrender if their white friends would write letters to Washington requesting arrangements for their defense. An unparalleled compact was then made between Johnson and Bgwo'ettin in which the elderly Navajo would return temporarily to the safety of Black Mesa to recover, in return for an assurance that he would go to Flagstaff and submit to the legal justice of the whites when notified of the trial date.[16]

A large number of Navajos were restless, convinced that the army was on the way to round them up, and they prepared to raid Flagstaff. One night about 300 well-armed Indians crossed the river north of Canyon Diablo at Wolf Post (built before 1870 by former mountain trapper Herman Wolf). Several of the leaders entered the store to seek advice from S. I. Richardson, a Navajo trader who ran the post. After hearing their story, Richardson was convinced that the evidence would not justify holding any of them for trial, although he warned there would be a hearing. His advice was that only a few ride into Flagstaff to return the horses and saddles taken from the scene of the fight and to confer with civil authorities.

The band of Navajos departed and decided on the way to hide in the pine forest above Flagstaff while the headmen presented themselves. If their leaders were jailed, the rest resolved to raid and burn the small town. The matter turned out the way Richardson thought it would, as he was told by the returning band two nights later.[17]

On February 24, 1900, Navajo Agent Hayzlett revealed that warrants for the arrest of the Navajos had been placed in his hands with a request that they be turned over to the proper authorities in Flagstaff. He was reluctant to carry out the request prior to the opening of court, set for April 9.

In March U.S. Attorney Robert E. Morrison, assigned to defend the Navajos, and District Attorney James Loy agreed that the defendants did not have to appear until a grand jury indicted them. A true bill was returned in April, and by August two of the defendants, Tohi'begay and Ada'ki'atsosi, had been surrendered to Sheriff Johnson.[18] Only Bgwo'ettin remained at large.

Two weeks before court convened in December 1899, Reverend

Johnston dispatched a courier to advise Bgwo'ettin of the day that the trial was scheduled to start. Opening day passed, but the old headman did not appear. He was still absent on the second day when Johnston was summoned before the grand jury to explain why he had counseled Bgwo'ettin to remain in hiding. He asked them to delay action one more day on an indictment charging him with aiding and abetting in the escape of the defendant.

On the third day of the trial, September 21, 1900, the still ailing Bgwo'ettin ended a grueling horseback ride from Black Mesa to Flagstaff with a dramatic entry into the courtroom, fully expecting to be sentenced to death on the gallows. The *Coconino Sun* described the scene: "The old man, over 70 years old, came accompanied by two other Indians, unexpectedly. Bowed down with years and suffering from the wounds of a bullet that passed through his entire body, he elbowed his way through the crowd and passed within the railing before the court."[19]

Judge Richard E. Sloan interrupted the proceedings and directed an interpreter to inquire who the intruder was and what business he had before the court. After the identity of the aged Navajo was revealed, and the fact of his ninety-mile ride to keep his word to appear in court, the judge ordered Bgwo'ettin to remain in the courtroom until the trial under way was concluded. Before the day ended the jury acquitted the two defendants on trial, and Judge Sloan promptly entered an order dismissing the case against Bgwo'ettin.[20]

Organized hostilities between cowboys and Navajos in northern Arizona were over.

10

Sheriff Frank Wattron's
International Furor

FRANK J. WATTRON and the Hash Knife outfit arrived in Holbrook at the same time. The Missouri-born drifter opened a drugstore next door to the saloon that was later called the Bucket of Blood. In a short time he added his own bar in the rear of his building. Wattron held seven official positions at once: justice of the peace, deputy sheriff, notary public, deputy clerk of court, deputy recorder, court commissioner, and school trustee.[1]

On one occasion, when he was serving as justice of the peace, a train carrying a large number of black soldiers made its regular stop in Holbrook. One of the soldiers got into a fight and was arrested by the local constable while the train was at the station.

Wattron was busy in his drugstore when the lawman brought in the offender. He continued to work in his typical judicial informality while the soldier confessed to a charge of disturbing the peace. When asked if he had any money, the defendant replied that he had about twenty dollars. Wattron ordered him to pay the whole sum to the constable and get the hell out of the store before the train left without him. Later, when recording the case, Wattron asked the arresting officer what the name of the defendant was. "Dam' 'f I know," answered the constable.

Wattron mumbled as he continued to write: "*Territory of Arizona* vs. *Damfino*, defendant."[2]

Rebuilding the town of Holbrook after the 1888 fire. A tent (*left center*) serves as a temporary saloon. The building to its left, still under construction, will house the Bucket of Blood saloon. The next building to the left is F. J. Wattron Drugs & Notions. Cowboys in the right center of the photograph loiter in front of the new A. & B. Schuster General Merchandise building. (National Archives)

Frank Wattron was an unpredictable character. One moment he could be grim, sinister, and given to vile language, the next kind and gentle-spoken, the latter a possible result of his use of laudanum, an opium-alcohol solution prescribed for pain and sleeplessness.

Wattron was a deputy sheriff in Apache County, Arizona, during the two-year term of Sheriff Commodore P. Owens in 1886–87. It was his duty to keep the peace and tame the rowdy cowboys in Holbrook while Owens was busy in other areas of the county.

Western writer Dane Coolidge told a story of a cowboy named Jackson, who, bolstered by a few drinks, announced in the Bucket of Blood that he was going to kill the local deputy. Wattron heard about the threat and picked up his menacing shotgun. When he entered the saloon through the back door, his "deep-set black eyes gleamed ferociously" and "he had his teeth skinned." He made the cowboy drop his gun and ordered him outside to meet his doom. The saloon received its name from earlier bloodshed that took place inside, but on this occasion the lawman did not want to "dirty the floor," as he put it. Outside, he drew a circle in the dusty street in which he made the cowboy stand and undergo a lengthy tongue-lashing. Finally, the lawman broke open his shotgun and showed the subdued braggart both barrels. They were empty.[3]

Frank J. Wattron, first sheriff of Navajo County, Arizona Territory. Photo made in Loui Ghuey Photograph Gallery, Holbrook. (Photo no. 43892, Arizona Historical Society Library, Tucson)

Coolidge told another story about Wattron and a Hash Knife cowboy he identified only by a last name, Haskins. (During the time Wattron was a deputy under Sheriff Owens, a cowboy named F. N. Haskell worked for the company. Haskins and Haskell were probably one and the same.) Wattron and the cowboy became involved in a standoff when the latter refused to put up his hands after being told to do so. Not wanting to kill the nervy young man just for being an all-night carouser, Wattron gave him a half hour to holster his gun.

The next morning, Wattron complained to Sheriff Owens that he needed help and, to his surprise, was authorized to pick another deputy. About that time, Haskins and his pals rode by on their way out of town back to the Hash Knife wagon. When Wattron hailed the dauntless cowboy who had stood up to him during the night and offered him a job as a deputy, it was accepted on the spot.[4] But the job must have been short lived, for by March 1887, Wattron himself was released because the sheriff could not afford to pay $25 a month for his services as a deputy in Holbrook.[5]

In November 1896, Wattron became the first elected sheriff and assessor of newly created Navajo County. He defeated John T. Jones, superintendent of the Aztec Land and Cattle Company, by seven votes.[6]

Trouble with cattle rustlers while he was manager of the Hash Knife was the principal reason Jones had decided to run for sheriff. While electioneering, the candidate was slapped and cursed by Bill Young, a renegade Mormon and well-known rustler. Jones made the mistake of declining to fight, as required by Western standards, and was defeated in the election.

The tall, dark, and thin Sheriff Wattron was striking in his physical appearance, sporting a long "snaky" black moustache and carrying a double-barreled sawed-off shotgun under a long frock coat that had a silver star pinned on its left side. A friend, C. O. Anderson of the *Holbrook Argus*, called him "the beau ideal sheriff of Navajo county."[7]

When Wattron returned to Holbrook from an extended deer and turkey hunt with Hash Knife superintendent Burt Mossman, one of his first duties was to send out invitations to the public hanging of a convicted murderer, scheduled for December 8, 1899. The Arizona penal code required the procedure to ensure the presence of witnesses, but the language and form of the invitation were left to the discretion of the county sheriff involved. The wording of Wattron's invitation caused such a negative reaction in the national and international press that the sheriff commented in retrospect that he got a "hell of a lot of Notoriety" out of it.[8]

The condemned man, George Smiley, had shot Thomas K. McSweeney on Monday, March 27, 1899, in Winslow.[9] McSweeney was a section foreman on the railroad with whom Smiley had argued a few days before about a shortage in his pay. McSweeney was not at fault because his former boss had the section hand entered in the time book for one day less than the man claimed he had worked.

On the day of the shooting, McSweeney was in town with his family to catch the train to Santa Fe where his wife, legally blind, was to be treated by a specialist. Smiley caught up with the new foreman at the depot. A heated conversation developed in which several blows were exchanged. As McSweeney attempted to leave the scene, Smiley shot him in the back.[10] Railroad employees placed the wounded man on a cot, and a local doctor treated him. When the train arrived, McSweeney was placed aboard and sent to the company hospital in Albuquerque, accompanied by his family.[11]

George Smiley was apprehended by Frank Wallace, Hash Knife range foreman, and held until the sheriff arrived to take custody.[12] The day after the shooting, Wattron went to Winslow, picked up Smiley, and took him to the county jail in Holbrook. McSweeney died at 3:40 the following morning, Wednesday, March 29, in the Albuquerque hospital.[13]

The murder case of the *Territory of Arizona vs. George Smiley* came up in the October term of court in Holbrook with Circuit Judge Richard E. Sloan presiding. On Friday, October 13, the defendant refused counsel and pled guilty to murder in the first degree. After reviewing all the evidence in the case, Judge Sloan had no other choice than to affix the death penalty to the offense. He sentenced Smiley to be hanged on the second Friday in December 1899.[14]

Friends of Sheriff Frank Wattron "joked, bantered, chafed, and quizzed" him about the nature of the hanging invitations and what he would say.[15] With what Judge Sloan called a "perverted sense of humor,"[16] Wattron drafted an invitation that fulfilled the anticipation of his supporters for something odd.

Lacking the printing equipment to do a proper job, C. O. Anderson of the *Holbrook Argus* forwarded the Wattron order for fifty invitations to the job printing department of the Albuquerque *Daily Citizen*.[17] It was through the perfidy of that office that the contents became known throughout the world.[18]

The hometown newspaper of Sheriff Wattron admitted a grim humor in the remarkably worded card and labeled it "a weird invitation." After stating that the soul of the convicted murderer "would swing into eternity on December 8, 1899, at 2 p.m. sharp," the invitation assured spectators that the "latest improved methods in the art of scientific strangulation [would] be employed and everything possible . . . done to make the surroundings cheerful and the execution a success."[19] The white-paneled invitation cards, hand-dated December 1, 1899, were placed in white envelopes and mailed.

Within three days, the Wattron invitation to the hanging had gained national attention and was being commented upon "from the Atlantic to the Pacific and from Maine to Florida."[20] By the end of the week, the "shocking invitation" had been printed in the London *Times*, the *Berliner Taggblat*, and *Le Figaro* in Paris with unfavorable comments on "the brutality of one of the Governors in one of the American Provinces."[21] President William McKinley was outraged and summarily transmitted his feelings to Governor N. Oakes Murphy of the Territory of Arizona.

On Thursday, December 7, 1899, the day before the scheduled hanging of George Smiley, a thirty-day stay was granted by Governor Murphy because of the flippant language used by Sheriff Wattron in his invitations. The Albuquerque newspaper that brought the story to the attention of the world commented on the same day, "The murderer will not 'swing in the most approved strangulation fashion' to-morrow as has been so artistically advertised by Sheriff F. J. Wattron."[22]

A scathing editorial by Charles C. Randolph appeared the next

Holbrook, Arizona, *December 1* 1899.

Mr. *J. M. Pratt*.

You are hereby cordially invited to attend the hanging of one

George Smiley, Murderer.

His soul will be swung into eternity on December 8, 1899, at 2 o'clock p. m., sharp.

The latest improved methods in the art of scientific strangulation will be employed and everything possible will be done to make the surroundings cheerful and the execution a success.   F. J. WATTRON,
Sheriff of Navajo County.

day in the influential *Arizona Republican* in which the editor and publisher condemned Sheriff Wattron for the great injury brought to the territory by the coarseness of his language and actions. The newspaper demanded a more sensitive approach by the sheriff to the solemn proceedings: "It will be necessary for the sheriff of Navajo county to issue a fresh invitation, and if he considers his best interests he will make it conform to the rule which governs similar proceedings in all civilized communities. The day of Arizona's 'rawness' is passing, and the sooner men like Wattron are made to appreciate the fact the better it will be for the credit of the territory."[23]

The *Holbrook Argus* came to the defense of Sheriff Wattron:

> Every man, woman and child throughout the confines of this county are acquainted with the generosity, tenderheartedness and unquestionable integrity of Sheriff Wattron. His official career has been unsurpassed in the section. As an officer he is absolutely without a peer in the West. Firm and fearless, yet kind and absolutely honest, he enjoys the respect of friends and foe. Higher officials in Arizona, with few exceptions, might copy a number of things from the conduct of the sheriff's office of Navajo county with profit. If every public office in this territory has been so efficiently and honestly conducted as the sheriff's office of Navajo county during Wattron's ad-

Revised Statutes of Arizona, Penal Code, Title X., Sec. 1849, Page 807, makes it obligatory on Sheriff to issue invitations to executions, form (unfortunately) not prescribed.

Holbrook, Arizona, 1/7— 1900.

Mr. *J. M. Pratt*

With feelings of profound sorrow and regret, I hereby invite you to attend and witness the private, decent and humane execution of a human being; name, George Smiley; crime, murder.

The said George Smiley will be executed on January 8, 1900, at 2 o'clock p. m.

You are expected to deport yourself in a respectful manner, and any "flippant" or "unseemly" language or conduct on your part will not be allowed. Conduct, on anyone's part, bordering on ribaldry and tending to mar the solemnity of the occasion will not be tolerated.

F. J. WATTRON,
Sheriff of Navajo County.

I would suggest that a committee, consisting of Governor Murphy, Editors Dunbar, Randolph and Hull, wait on our next legislature and have a form of invitation to executions embodied in our laws.

ministration, when their official history shall be written, there will be no thievery to record, and no official dishonesty or incompetency to smooth over and excuse.[24]

Bowing to the pressure of the president of the United States, the governor of the Arizona Territory, and several Arizona newspaper editors, Wattron wrote another invitation to the hanging of George Smiley, but once again he did it his way. The rewritten invitation was headed and closed with sarcastic comments by the sheriff in fine print. At the top of the message was the statement that the Revised Statutes of Arizona made it obligatory on the sheriff to issue invitations to executions with a standard form "(unfortunately) not pre-scribed."

In the newly worded invitation, Sheriff Wattron announced "with profound sorrow and regret" the execution of George Smiley, to take place on January 8, 1900, at 2 P.M. A warning was given that no "flippant" or "unseemly" language would be allowed and that "con-duct bordering on ribaldry and tending to mar the solemnity of the occasion" would not be tolerated. At the bottom was a postscript by the sheriff telling his critics what he thought they should do: "I would suggest that a committee consisting of Governor Murphy, Editors Dunbar, Randolph and Hull, wait on our next Legislature and have a form of invitation to executions embodied in our laws." As a gesture of mourning, Wattron had the new invitations edged with a quarter-inch black border. They were hand-dated January 7, 1900, and enclosed in matching black-bordered envelopes. They were not mailed until the following day, however, when Wattron was sure they would not be received by the governor and other officials until the execution had been carried out.[25]

George Smiley was converted to the Catholic faith and baptized by Father Felix Dilly of Flagstaff on the Sunday night before his execution on Friday. He spoke little about his past but did reveal that he was born in Ohio and drifted to Montana at the age of seventeen. He claimed to have a brother still living in Montana. Smiley was about thirty-seven years old, five feet eight inches tall, and about 180 pounds. He was strong and muscular and had light hair and blue eyes.

Promptly at 2 P.M. on January 8, 1900, Sheriff Wattron, Deputy Joe Bargman, and Father Dilly ascended the scaffold with the doomed killer. When asked if he had anything to say, Smiley re-plied: "I have nothing to say except to thank the Sheriff and his deputies for courtesies, and I die a Christian." The trap was sprung and Smiley dropped to his death. The hanging was witnessed by about a dozen spectators, most of whom were outsiders.[26]

Burt Mossman did not attend the execution in spite of having been teased about going or not going by his friend Sheriff Wattron. The Hash Knife boss later recalled: "I remember well as Frank came back from the court house, where Smiley had just been hung, the sheriff threw down a piece of rope he had just cut from the hangman's noose, and told me he wanted me to have something to remember him by."[27]

Frank Wattron died from an overdose of laudanum on August 2, 1905, at the age of forty-four. The custodian of the courthouse and other county personnel walked the sheriff back and forth for hours in an unsuccessful attempt to work off the effects of the deadly drug. Just before Wattron died, he reportedly told those who had tried to save his life, "Well, boys, I have a ticket punched straight to Hell, with no stop-overs."[28]

11

The Babbitt Era of the
Hash Knife in Arizona

THE first pioneers to engage in the cattle business on a large scale in the Flagstaff area of northern Arizona were John W. Young, a son of Brigham Young, and Lot Smith, a Mormon church official. They were followed by the Babbitt brothers of Cincinnati, who established a business of epic proportions, buying the Hash Knife brand in the process.

In the summer of 1880, Young secured a grading and tie contract for the building of the railroad through the area. He built a construction camp below Leroux Springs at the foot of the San Francisco Mountains in what is now Fort Valley, nine miles north of Flagstaff.

Resenting the building of the "iron trail," Navajos and Apaches raided construction gangs almost daily along its route. Young and his workers heard that a large war party was planning an attack on the headquarters and hastily began to erect a fort for defense. The stockade, seventy feet wide by one hundred feet long, was built in record time. When the war party heard the fort was heavily fortified and well manned, they abandoned their plans. The stockade was named Fort Moroni to honor the Mormon angel.[1]

With the completion of his contract with the railroad company, and the threat of attacks diminished, Young established the Moroni Cattle Company. In 1883, in association with Eastern capitalists, he helped to organize the Arizona Cattle Company. The stockade walls

A herd of A One Bar cattle rounded up for branding at Leroux Springs one mile from Fort Rickerson, the old home ranch. (Earle Forrest Collection, Museum of Northern Arizona, Flagstaff)

of the fort were cut down to fence height, other buildings erected, and the name changed to Fort Rickerson in honor of Charles L. Rickerson, an official of the new corporation. The huge cattle operation, claiming a range of 875 square miles from Clark Valley north to the Grand Canyon and from the Little Colorado west to Ash Fork, became known by its brand name, the A One Bar. The company had a legal title to only 132,000 acres that had been purchased from the Atlantic and Pacific Railroad Company. Two years later, Young left the area permanently after a warrant was issued charging him with polygamy.[2]

Lot Smith was one of the first Mormon settlers in northern Arizona where he arrived in 1876. He settled first at Sunset on the Little Colorado River and became the head of that settlement in addition to those at St. Joseph, Brigham City, and Obed.

Smith established his Circle S ranch and dairy at Mormon Lake, sixty miles west of Sunset, in September 1878. In the late 1880s, he moved to an oasis in the Painted Desert known later as Tuba City. The Smith cattle interests sprawled from Mormon Lake on the south to Tuba City on the north. One Mormon historian wrote, "His tenacity and toughness were . . . demonstrated by his ability to

The A One Bar cattle headquarters seen from the south, photographed in the early 1890s, with the San Francisco Mountains as a backdrop. The side-by-side six-room cabin of the original Fort Moroni is on the left. The room with the porch roof was used as the ranch kitchen. A large barn and various other outbuildings, including the commissary, are visible. Also noticeable in places are the stockade crossties cut down to fence height. (Photo no. 28039, Arizona Historical Society Library, Tucson)

hang on in a country which by this time was the preserve of the great Aztec Land and Cattle Company."[3]

Smith's eldest son remained at Mormon Lake, the center of the family stock-raising activities. By crossing imported Kentucky stallions with Arizona range mares, Smith developed a strain of saddle horses with the necessary speed and stamina for his frequent 260-mile round-trips, by way of Flagstaff, between the distant points of his business.

The cattle-raising potential in northern Arizona in the late 1880s attracted two Babbitt brothers from Cincinnati, who had a mere $20,000 to invest. Along with three other brothers who arrived later, they were to establish a cattle and mercantile dynasty.

The two brothers' concern about available pasture rights in the area was lessened somewhat by a Flagstaff resident who told them that, after they obtained water rights, they had the whole northern end of the territory on which to run cattle: "You just turn them loose—after you put your brand on them, of course. In the spring and fall you round them up, along with your neighbors, sort out the cattle that are yours, and ship them to market."[4] While looking for a ranch site, the Babbitt brothers met local ranching partners Al Grady and Jack Smith who had grazing land and a source of water north of town, both of which they leased to the prospective cattlemen.[5]

On April 10, 1886, the Flagstaff newspaper reported that David and William Babbitt were the guests of townsman Dr. D. J. Brennen while they shopped for cattle.[6] Within two weeks, the brothers had bought a fine herd bunched near Walnut Canyon that had been driven from Arkansas City, Kansas, by owners John Hosler and Drury Warren. A notice in the *Arizona Champion* overstated the number of cattle in the deal at 1,200 head.[7]

The original bill of sale was not signed until April 30. The transfer actually involved 613 cows, 128 two-year-olds, 96 yearlings, and 27 bulls, a total of 864 head. Included also were 19 good cowponies. The cost of $20 a head took almost all the money the brothers had. A Texas cowboy named Sam French, the range boss of the Hosler and Warren herd, went with the deal. Acting on his advice, the Babbitt brothers had the old Boot brand of the herd barred out within three weeks and replaced by the C O Bar, a sentimental reminder of their home town, Cincinnati, Ohio.[8] Horses in the purchase wore a Jug brand.

During the first summer, the initial Babbitt herd ranged high in the San Francisco Mountains where the waters of Jack Smith Spring flowed into the mountain pastures from the inner basin of the peaks. The cattle wanted to move continually, forcing the Babbitt brothers

The pioneer Babbitt brothers in Arizona. *Left to right:* George (1860–1920), Charles J. (1865–1956), Edward (1867–1943), William (1862–1930), and David (1858–1929). (Arizona Historical Society, Flagstaff)

and their cowboys to sleep on the trail at night to keep them contained.[9] When winter came, the cattle were driven down to a range along the Little Colorado River near Grand Falls.

At the end of the second year, the Babbitt cattle were moved south to Pump House Wash, eight miles below Flagstaff. The Babbitts purchased the Clark Valley ranch and what was left of the John Clark cattle. Headquarters was then moved to John Clark Spring near Lake Mary, fifteen miles southeast of Flagstaff.[10]

Within a month after David and William Babbitt entered the cattle business, their brother Charles J., better known later as "Mr. C. J.," joined them. Early in 1887, another brother, George, moved to Flagstaff and became a bookkeeper before joining his brothers in their broadening business ventures. When beef prices dropped in 1887, David left the ranch in Clark Valley and opened the first Babbitt store in Flagstaff. Despite adversity, William and C. J.

Barnett (Barney) Stiles (1867–1914), Hash Knife cowboy in Texas and Arizona. Stiles rounded up the remnants of the Hash Knife herds after the liquidation of the Aztec Land and Cattle Company and became part owner of the brand with the Babbitt Brothers Trading Company. (Courtesy of Mary M. Bailey)

maintained the cattle business.[11] One writer described the dedication of the former midwestern grocers: "Billy and C. J. were squarely in the middle of the operation all the way—expending their sweat and sometimes their blood, freezing in winter and sweltering in summer, wallowing in manure, and breathing in the acrid smell of branding iron on calf hide."[12] Edward Babbitt joined his four brothers in 1890 but returned to Cincinnati after serving briefly as a probate judge and for one term in the Territorial Legislature.

Meanwhile, the Navajos came to resent bitterly the Mormon settlement of Lot Smith at Tuba City. On June 20, 1892, the famed Mormon leader was shot to death by Navajos in the remoteness of Moencopi Wash after he killed several of their sheep that were grazing in his alfalfa fields.[13] His Circle S ranch and Mormon Dairy were then purchased by the Babbitt brothers. Then, following the failure of the Arizona Cattle Company in 1899, the ever-expanding Babbitt enterprises bought the A One Bar stock and brand the following year.

On October 12, 1899, the Arizona Cattle Company sold its timber and grazing lands for $140,000, to William F. Baker, trustee of the Manistee Lumber Company.[14] The Michigan-based company later merged with the Saginaw Lumber Company and began harvesting northern Arizona timber.

Certain parcels of grazing land that had been leased to the Arizona Cattle Company by the Saginaw Lumber Company were purchased on December 23, 1902, by David Babbitt for the Babbitt enterprises.[15] Instead of the vast unbroken block of rangeland once controlled by the A One Bar, the Babbitt purchases were divided into three main ranging areas—the Cedar Springs range, the Little Springs range, and the Fort Valley range.[16] The new owners abandoned Fort Rickerson in 1904 when a summer ranch was established at the old Bucklar place on Hart Prairie, high up on the western slope of the San Francisco Mountains.

A continuation of the Hash Knife saga was assured in the spring of 1902, when the Babbitts, in partnership with former Hash Knife cowboy Barney Stiles, purchased for $3,000 both the brand and remnant cattle from the Aztec Land and Cattle Company.[17] The existence of the brand in the territory spanned two periods of ownership and management. Under absentee ownership from 1884 until

George W. Hennessey in 1911, when he was thirty-three years old. When he died in 1973 at the age of ninety-five, he was the last living Hash Knife cowboy who worked for the Aztec Land and Cattle Company. (J. & W. Seligman Co. Archives, Bass Business Collection, University of Oklahoma, Norman)

1900, the cattle outfit had a reputation of being overridden with both raw and seasoned hotheads. When under resident ownership, beginning in 1902, the cowboys' overall conduct changed for the better.

George W. Hennessey worked for the Hash Knife during the transition period, from 1899 to 1901. When he died in 1973 at the age of ninety-five, Hennessey was credited with being the last living Hash Knife cowboy who had worked for the historic Aztec Land and Cattle Company.[18] It made him bristle when someone called the company "that Hashknife outlaw outfit." Some of the cowboys who worked with him became leading citizens, and a few were elected to county offices. Still, he admitted that "the Hashknife no doubt had some poor characters as they worked from 25 to 30 men from April 1st to November 15."[19]

No land was involved in the Stiles-Babbitt purchase. Stiles organized numerous roundups for previously overlooked cattle that still survived in the remote recesses, mountains, and canyons, "the old mossback steers and cows that were wild as panthers and just as cagey." He had helped drive an early Hash Knife herd from the Pecos River north into New Mexico, and from there he accompanied them by rail to Arizona. Stiles had no first name as a boy but was simply called Bud. When he was nineteen years old, he selected the name Barnett, and his friends called him Barney from then on.[20]

On May 7, 1902, the Aztec Land and Cattle Company relinquished thousands of acres of land, within the limits of the San Francisco Mountains Forest Reserve in Coconino County, to the United States in exchange for an equal quantity of public lands

The chuck box on a Hash Knife wagon given to the Navajo County Museum by descendants of George W. Hennessey. (Photo by the author)

elsewhere. The deeds were signed in the offices of the corporation in New York City by Albert Strauss, first vice president.[21]

The former Esperanza Ranch of Will Barnes, located in Section 26 on Chevelon Creek, which flows into the Little Colorado River twelve miles east of Winslow, was bought by Barney Stiles and Charles J. Babbitt on January 24, 1903. Included in the purchase was an additional pasture and corral fifteen miles south of the ranch, between Rocky Canyon and Black Canyon, known as the Black Canyon Pasture.[22]

Disorderly conduct by cowboys working for Stiles and Babbitt seldom made the newspapers, but some former employees of the parent Aztec Land and Cattle Company continued to be in the news. They had already helped establish a reputation of unbridled lawlessness for all Hash Knife cowboys, and for a time it became the reputation also of those who worked for the new owners of the brand. A Winslow historian sums up the scenario of how the earlier ones dictated the poor esteem in which the parent company was held: "A good many did not last long on the Company payroll but were ever after known as Hash Knife cowboys and whatever trouble they were involved in was piled high at the door of the Aztec Company, along with that of the incorrigible and uncontrolled conditions which were the lot of most absentee ranch ownership in the West."[23]

Lucien Creswell and Tex Roxy were having drinks at the end of the bar in the Wigwam Saloon in Winslow around 1:30 A.M. on Saturday, April 8, 1905, when John Shaw and a man who called himself William Smith bellied up to the bar and ordered drinks. The former Hash Knife cowboys paid little attention to the late-comers at first. A bottle and glasses were placed before the two. One poured the whiskey and tossed down some money. Neither touched his drink.[24] This inaction on their part would be a significant factor in an unbelievable chain of events that happened over the next three days.

Creswell noticed one of the late customers (both said to have been Hash Knife boys) place his hand on the arm of the other to get his attention. Together they stared at the stacks of silver dollars where gaming attendant Frank Ketchum was running a dice game. Then, according to Creswell, in typical laconic cowboy form, "They drew guns and went over and held up the game."[25] Their pockets bulging with coins, the robbers backed out of the saloon onto Third Street, leaving their full glasses on the bar. They also left a trail of silver dollars.

Deputy Sheriff J. N. (Pete) Pemberton, owner of the Wigwam Saloon, gambler, and former Hash Knife cowboy, was summoned. He and Town Marshal Joe Giles searched the alleys for signs that might indicate where the robbers had left their horses. The two lawmen came out on Front Street. While crossing the railroad embankment on the way to the opposite side of the street, Pemberton spied a silver dollar reflecting the bright moonlight. More coins were found as the officers moved west along the tracks. They picked up six more at the end of the crossties where scuffed-up boot marks in the dirt indicated that the robbers had probably boarded a slow-moving freight train that had just come through.[26]

Notified by Pemberton, Sheriff C. I. (Chet) Houck arrived from Holbrook, and the two took the next train west toward Flagstaff. Upon reaching Canyon Diablo, the officers consulted with Sheriff Ed Henderson of Coconino County, who had worked his way east after being notified of the robbery. The three decided that Houck and Pemberton would backtrack toward Winslow while Henderson

looked for the robbers from Canyon Diablo west.[27] En route back to
Winslow, Sheriff Houck was informed that a brakeman had seen
two men hiding behind some brush one mile east of Canyon Diablo.[28] When the train reached the small wayside station at Sunshine,
the two officers got off, secured their horses, and headed back.

Around 6:30 P.M., Fred Volz, owner of a trading post on the north
side of the tracks at Canyon Diablo, saw Houck and Pemberton
approaching from the east. Knowing the officers were after the robbers, he called to them with a warning that two strange men were in
the section house.[29] A few moments later, the robbers emerged and
began walking west toward a large red warehouse that belonged to
Volz. The officers headed for the front end of the building at the
same time the robbers disappeared from sight behind the far end.
Houck and Pemberton made their way to the near corner of the
warehouse and suddenly came face to face with the wanted men.
Gladwell Richardson, who interviewed participants and witnesses,
commented, "Just as the aftermath bred a bizarre and incredible
episode, so did the amazing shootout that followed in the bat of an
eye. Weird to say the least, both incidents are probably the most
unusual ever occurring in the west."[30]

The four men faced each other at a distance said to be under six
feet and fired twenty-one shots from their handguns. Neither officer

was hit, but Pemberton had a bullet hole in his coat sleeve near the right shoulder. Smith suffered two serious wounds. Three of the shots taken at Shaw by the sheriff hit their mark before the lawman ran out of bullets. With his final shot, Shaw fired point-blank at the sheriff at the precise moment Pemberton leveled him, causing Shaw's bullet to go astray. Pemberton was the only one of the four who had a full cylinder in his six-shooter instead of the customary five cartridges carried by gunmen for safety reasons. This extra bullet struck Shaw in the side of the head.[31] Even though it was Pemberton's bullet that killed Shaw, Houck took the responsibility because he was sheriff.[32]

The wounded Smith moved as fast as he could toward the west switch before he sat down and gave himself up. According to the testimony of Volz, Smith made the following statement at an inquest held later that evening: "My name is W. Smith you do not need to look for anyone else We took the money I had $154.00 and Shaw had $117.00—We intended to take the guns away from the officers and walk away." He added that he and Shaw were both good shots and he was surprised the officers were not hit.[33] In an effort to clarify his last name, he was asked if it was spelled S-m-i-t-h. "No," he answered, "S-m-y-t-h-e."[34]

Within two hours, Sheriff Henderson, in whose county the shoot-out occurred, and John Harrington, justice of the peace and ex officio coroner, arrived from Flagstaff on a train. A jury was empaneled on the scene with Fred Volz as foreman. Their verdict was that John Shaw, deceased, died by "Gun Shot in the Hands of C. I. Houck, Sheriff of Navajo Co. Ariz. in his official duty and we exonerate him."[35] Shaw was hastily buried on the south side of the tracks in a long pine box from the stock Volz kept at his trading post for Navajo burials.

Back in Winslow the following night, April 9, a number of cowboys in the Wigwam Saloon were voicing their contempt for Sheriff Houck and even criticizing him for not giving a drink of liquor to the slain robber before he buried him. At least six Hash Knife boys got in on the discussion, the most vocal of whom was Sam Case. He was drinking heavily, but so was everyone else.

Sam wanted to know if it was true the robbers had paid for drinks the night before that they never even tasted. Some said they bought

Frank Ketchum, Hosteen Chi (Navajo), Tom Hesser, Bill Campbell, and Young Marley stand above John Shaw's grave after it was uncovered. Even in death, Shaw appeared to welcome the delayed drink. These four remarkable photographs were first owned by Sam Case, who was present at the proceedings. He gave them to W. H. Burbage, Winslow merchant and attorney, who kept them until

whiskey and drank it, but the bartender stated positively that they paid for two drinks and left them on the bar untouched. Joe Giles strolled in about that time and someone asked him what he thought about a man going to his grave thirsty. His answer was that everybody in the saloon had too much "red eye" in them and they all needed to go somewhere and sleep it off.[36]

After Giles left, the conversation dragged on until Sam Case proposed that they go dig up Shaw and give him a drink even though he was in no condition to enjoy it. A number of those present agreed. About that time the whistle of a westbound train sounded, and Ed Rogers urged the revelers to hurry out and catch a ride to Canyon Diablo. At least twenty-five men, including Rogers, ran for the railroad yard, but only fifteen made it in time to get aboard, Pete Pemberton and Frank Ketchum among them.

The boisterous group arrived at Canyon Diablo at dawn and bor-

Frank Ketchum

rowed shovels from a reluctant Fred Volz. He handed them a Kodak box camera and said to get the sheriff a picture for identification purposes in case Shaw was a wanted man. The party then moved south across the tracks to the *camp santo* where Shaw reposed. The dirt was heaved away from the grave and the lid pried off the wooden box. There lay Shaw with a faint smile on his face.

"The group crowded around the grave in utter silence," wrote Gladwell Richardson. "Shaw's death wound had not disfigured the head as a lead bullet usually did on spreading to break the brain box. Some of the Hashknife cowboys were near outlaws themselves, and a few had been run out of Texas as outlaws. Perhaps during the minutes thay gazed down into the open grave their past arose before them, and except for a little luck in time one of them might have been the young man in the crude casket. Perhaps there had been malice in some of them at the outset of the strange quest, the proposal to dig up the dead man and give him a drink. But now there were few dry eyes among them." The sight of John Shaw lying there in the opened pine box, disturbed in his eternal rest, had a sobering effect on the cowboys. It was now a solemn occasion. Jack LeBarron, one of the Hash Knife boys present, recalled nearly thirty years later that it was no longer a "joking expedition." "There's some folks called us grave robbers afterwards, drunken ghouls for digging him up," he said. "But then and there it seemed to us that giving him a drink for his last trail was proper."[37]

Sam Case and Bill Campbell dropped down in the hole and lifted the body up. Once out of the grave, the corpse was stood up against a picket fence that surrounded another burial plot. The cowboys moved about in almost complete silence. Two of them held Shaw and poured a drink from a long-necked whiskey bottle through teeth that were already locked behind a haunting death grin. Then he was lowered back into the box. Young Marley sang two verses of "Bringing in the Sheaves" and said a childhood prayer. All the while Ezra Hayes was snapping pictures of the grim proceedings. The unfinished bottle of whiskey was dropped into the box and the lid replaced. As the grave was covered for the second time, the dull thuds of dirt and stones wafted across the bleak landscape. The cowboys then ambled over to the depot where an early morning train was due.

William Smith, or Smythe, was tried in Holbrook and sentenced to the Territorial Prison in Yuma on October 12, 1905, after pleading guilty to armed robbery. Upon his arrival at the prison four days later, it was determined that his real name was William Evans, and that he was a former inmate who had served six years of a ten-year sentence for robbery and had been out only two years. For the Canyon Diablo robbery, Evans was paroled on April 1, 1914, and his citizenship was restored a few months later.[38]

Exactly two weeks after William Evans, alias William Smith, arrived at prison, Peter Pemberton was involved in another fatal shooting. Around 7:30 P.M. on October 28, 1905, the part-time Navajo County deputy shot and killed Town Marshal Joe Giles, who had assisted him in the search for the Wigwam Saloon robbers.[39] The killing also helped end the career of Sheriff C. I. Houck.

Pemberton had been drinking and gambling at the Parlor Saloon on Front Street across from the railroad depot in Winslow. After losing a considerable amount of money, he went back over to his own gambling emporium, the Wigwam Saloon, where he got $50 more and returned.[40] Testimony brought out at the delayed trial revealed that when Pemberton got back he started gambling again at a roulette table run by Walter Darling. Pemberton became enraged when Darling would not allow him to place a bet on the number 13. He stepped back, pulled his gun, and threatened the life of the house man. Joe Giles had just entered the saloon on one of his nightly rounds when the altercation began. He stepped up behind Pemberton and asked him not to cause trouble. The infuriated gambler wheeled and fired shots at the lawman; four struck him in the abdomen, three of which caused mortal wounds.[41]

Pemberton was not arrested, asked to give bail, committed to jail, or given a preliminary hearing. He was said to be indifferent about the whole affair and apparently had no fear of the consequences. Sheriff Houck was quoted as saying that he had no intention of making an arrest in the case because "Pemberton had saved his life some months earlier [at Canyon Diablo] by shooting a drunken cow puncher who was about to kill the sheriff."[42] (Houck ran for reelection in Navajo County and was defeated.)

On October 11, 1906, twelve months after the murder of Joe Giles, a felony indictment was filed against Pete Pemberton. Nearly two weeks later, he was granted a change of venue to Yavapai County. The defense for Pemberton at the trial attempted to show that he was crazed from a three-day drunk. Evidence offered by his attorney was that he had been severely injured in the head on two different occasions as a child and that this had a tendency to cause temporary insanity when his system was inflamed by overindulgence in alcohol. On December 5 it took the jury less than an hour to find Pemberton guilty of second-degree murder, and Judge Richard E. Sloan sentenced him to twenty-five years in the Territorial Prison in Yuma.[43] Ironically, he joined his former captive, William Evans (Smith), who had robbed his saloon and was already serving time.

Pete Pemberton did not serve his full sentence. In 1925 he was back with the Hash Knife as a horse wrangler at Stud Camp on the north side of the Little Colorado River near company headquarters. Mack Hughes, a fellow worker, described him as "a big red-faced man, weighing two hundred pounds, but he didn't look like he had an ounce of fat on him. I didn't like him though, because I believe he was the meanest man to a horse I ever saw."[44]

In 1906 the Babbitt brothers put up half the money for the purchase of what was to be called the Hart Cattle Company, which in time became another range for Hash Knife cattle. Leo F. Verkamp, a brother-in-law to three of the original Babbitt brothers, and D. Leslie (Les) Hart each took a quarter interest. The ranch, west of Winslow, was bought for $95,000 from William D. Roden. The brand was the well-known Pitchfork. The Hart cattle operation ran from Lake Mary east to Meteor Crater. It included 38,000 deeded acres, 31,000 acres under state leases, and grazing permits to 40,000 acres of Forest Service land.[45]

Barney Stiles sold out his interest in the Hash Knife irrigation

Mack Hughes on Scarface at Bootleg Still near Willow Creek in 1929. (Courtesy of Stella Hughes)

Edward Henry Bargman (1869–1947), part owner of the Hash Knife cattle operation from 1910 to 1914. (Bill Wyrick Collection)

system on Chevelon Creek—consisting of the dam and dam site, ditches, and laterals—to the Babbitts on March 16, 1910. Then, on December 20 of that year, he sold them his half interest in the ranch.[46] Stiles then went into partnership with his brother, Seth Rogers Stiles, and established the Johns Draw Ranch, twenty-five miles north of Winslow.[47]

The day after the Babbitts became sole owners of the Hash Knife range, they sold a quarter interest in it to Edward H. Bargman of Navajo County.[48] Bargman had gone to work for the nearby Waters Cattle Company when he was only sixteen years old. Before he bought into the Hash Knife operation, he and his brother Joe ran a small cattle outfit in the Tuba City country.[49]

Over the years it became customary for the Babbitts to buy into area cattle companies as copartners, retaining the original name and leaving the former owners in managerial positions. John G. Babbitt, son of C. J., represented the family in the cattle operations from the Great Depression through the Hash Knife era. He explained the company acquisitions: "It seemed that nearly everybody with as much as 50 acres or a dozen cattle started a cattle company and registered a brand. Many of them needed a partner with money, and various Babbitts entered into these partnerships. Other outfits ran

Heck Marley, assisted by his brothers, branding on the open range. (Old Trails Museum, Winslow, Arizona)

up bills with Babbitt Brothers and offered their ranches in payment. As a result, Babbitts took over dozens of cattle companies and their brands." In the forty years following the founding of the C O Bar in 1886, nearly one hundred brands came under Babbitt control. By the end of World War I, the giant corporation's ranches covered more than 3 million acres in Arizona, California, and Kansas.[50]

Following the Babbitts' acquisition of the Hart Ranch, their Pitchfork and Hash Knife cattle became the target of rustlers, disappearing at a rate of nearly 200 a month.[51] This began to happen in the summer of 1906, soon after Joseph W. ("Pop") Marley moved into the area from the Davis Mountains of West Texas with his family and 2,000 cattle.

Pop Marley was a diminutive man, standing only five feet two inches tall and weighing less than a hundred pounds, but he was infinitely imposing as a cattle rustler with one of the most unique court cases on record. The six Marley boys located the family ranch south of Winslow on Clear Creek. The range of their U Bar and L Prod cattle bordered part of the Babbitt cattle empire. The Marley parents and their six daughters settled in town.

Pop Marley went into the butchering business in Winslow in competition with the firm of Lyons and Spellmire, a Babbitt subsidiary, which up until that time had a monopoly on the meat business. When it was discovered that the Marleys were operating without a license, they were forced to close. They retaliated by building a slaughterhouse at their ranch headquarters on the rim of Jacks Canyon four miles from town and butchering cattle that did not belong to them. Offal and hides from the stolen cattle were dumped into the canyon stream through a trapdoor, in the hope that the brands could not be identified after being pounded in the rushing waters. Another way the Marleys obliterated brands was to toss the hides into pig pens and let the hogs root them over.

One of the Marley sons, Young Marley, was bookkeeper and general manager of the operation. Every animal killed was entered into his record books. Two columns were used to tally each of the family brands and a single dot in a third column, labeled "Profit Stuff," indicated that an animal had been rustled. Over 90 percent of the butchered cattle was said to have been stolen from the Hart Cattle Company, and only 10 percent came from the Marley herds.[52]

For five years, the unsuspecting Lyons and Spellmire purchased some of their own beef from the Marley slaughterhouse. The Marleys had become respected citizens in the county and Pop one of the wealthiest men in Winslow, but they were careless in their greed. Even though they were his friends, Les Hart, manager of the Hart Ranch and owner of a quarter interest in it, became suspicious of the Marleys because of the high number of his cattle that could not be accounted for and the increased financial prosperity of his neighbors. He hired Reuben L. (Rube) Neill, a former Arizona Ranger, as a range detective at $100 a month.[53]

Meanwhile, Young Marley had fallen out of grace with members of his family. On a trip to California, he spent a considerable amount of money on racehorses and was physically assaulted by the whole household when he returned. Ready and willing to spill the beans on the illegal operation, he secretly confessed to Les Hart to avoid prosecution.

Hart devised a plan to catch the other members of the family redhanded. The next morning, he rode out to the Marleys' and stayed for lunch. He told his hosts that he and his wife were leaving the next day to see some of her kinfolks on the Verde River and would spend the summer there. Back in town, he gave the same story to the local newspaper. He then told Lyons to order thirteen steers from the Marleys.

Two mornings later, Sheriff Joe Woods and his deputy, Hart, and Neill rode out to the Marley ranch under the cover of darkness. Hart and the sheriff entered Jacks Canyon below the slaughter pens and the other two came down the canyon. They picketed their horses and waited for daylight.

Hours later, the Pitchfork boss sighted the Marley boys driving fifteen head of cattle toward the corrals. He recognized the animals as his stock. Waiting patiently until one steer was killed, skinned, and quartered, the four closed in on the illegal operation. One of the Marley boys was headed for the trapdoor with the fresh hide when Hart ordered him at gunpoint to return with it. All of the rustlers surrendered peacefully.

The posse found that the Marleys had earlier thrown hides in deep cracks in the canyon walls and covered them with slaked lime to kill the odor. Many had Pitchfork or Hash Knife brands on them. Others were wrapped around big rocks, tied with baling wire, and dumped into the water. Deep potholes yielded over a hundred hides.[54]

Seventy-seven hides were impounded at the Marley slaughter-house and taken to Winslow where they were put to soak at the R. C. Creswell corral. Members of the Livestock Sanitary Board were ordered to prove the ownership of the hides. Of twenty-five examined in the first two days of the investigation, only four bore a Marley brand. Some local stockmen were quoted as saying the case looked serious for the prominent family.[55]

On May 7, 1912, a Navajo County grand jury indicted the Marleys on sixteen counts of grand larceny.[56] They were scheduled for

Above: Changing Hash Knife horses near Clear Creek Dam. *Right:* Charles Edgar Wyrick (1869–1938) and his wife, the former Mamie Jarvis, in 1905. Wyrick was co-owner of the Hash Knife with the Babbitts from 1914 until 1934. (Both photos from Bill Wyrick Collection)

Hash Knife cowboys washing in Big Tank, June 10, 1917. *Left to right:* ——Green, Jake Miller, Fred Creswell, and George Creswell. (Courtesy of Stella Hughes)

trial in Holbrook and hired two of the best attorneys in Arizona to defend them. Two other outstanding trial lawyers in the territory represented the plaintiffs. The Babbitts were active behind the scenes but conspicuously absent from the proceedings.

The Marley trial opened on October 23, 1912, with the prosecution based on an exhibit of seventy-seven hides bearing various brands.[57] The oratory of the distinguished Henry F. Ashurst, which had helped carry him to the U.S. Senate, held jury and bystanders spellbound as he argued for the defense. He ended his plea for an acquittal with well-chosen quotations from the Bible. A burst of cheers from the gallery when he sat down gave every indication of a favorable verdict for his clients.

A modest Reese M. Ling, one of the attorneys for the plaintiffs, made an immediate decision to neutralize the eloquence of the flamboyant Ashurst and stake the entire case on a single counteraction: "My brilliant and learned colleague," he began, "has presented a masterly argument for acquittal of the accused, Joseph Marley and his five sons. To reinforce his argument, he has quoted from the greatest of all books, the Holy Bible, but gentlemen of the jury, Mr. Ashurst has forgotten to tell you that one of the Ten Commandments is: 'Thou shalt not steal'. We are here to see that this commandment of holy writ is obeyed and this can only be done by convicting Joseph Marley and his sons."[58]

Heck, Clay, and Dee Marley were convicted, along with their father, and sentenced to serve not less than one year and no more than ten years. An appeal was filed immediately, but because Arizona had just become the forty-eighth state in the federal union the appeal was not heard until 1914. Subsequently, the defendants were granted a new trial by the state appellate court. It opened on July 17, 1914.

At a secret meeting during the second trial, Pop Marley and Les Hart, who had remained on friendly terms, agreed that the accused would pay $75,000 to cover the cost of the stolen cattle and plead guilty in return for a suspended sentence request by Hart on their behalf. With this understanding, the trial was concluded with five-year suspended sentences. The Winslow newspaper headlined the decision as "gladsome news."[59]

The Arizona Livestock Protective League presented Les Hart with a diamond ring in appreciation for his tenacity in the case. The disposition of the gift supplies an interesting postscript to the case. "Years later," wrote two Babbitt historians, "he was forced to hock it to get enough money to purchase a modest present for Pop and Mrs. Marley, who had invited him to attend their Golden Wedding Anniversary in California. Thus, in the twilight of their lives, the three old friends were reunited, the memory of those bitter years forgotten and diminished by the passage of time."[60] To cover his mounting indebtedness to the Babbitts, Hart was forced to relinquish his interest in the Hart Cattle Company in 1921.[61]

The Babbitts continued to accumulate Hash Knife assets. Ed Bargman, who was part owner of the Hash Knife outfit for just over three years, on March 11, 1914, sold half of his interest to his brother-in-law Charles E. Wyrick of Winslow and the other half to Charles J. Babbitt. Three days later, Bargman conveyed to Babbitt and Wyrick, by quit-claim deed, three water locations established on unsurveyed public lands of the United States: Sheet Rock Draw and dam between Clear Creek and Chevelon Creek; Fagan Draw at a point ten miles from Clear Creek on the way to Chevelon Creek; and a location on Clear Creek at the mouth of Sheep Corral Canyon, seven miles south of Winslow and a mile and a half southeast of Folsom's concrete dam on Jacks Canyon. Wyrick bought part of the water rights to the former Esperanza Ranch from Babbitt on March 23, 1914.[62]

The cattle operation of Babbitt and Wyrick during the early years was successful, and the prosperity of the overall Babbitt cattle involvement was never better. Their aggregate cattle sales peaked in 1915 when receipts totaled nearly $1.5 million. Income fell temporarily the next year, then came back during World War I, approaching the $1 million mark in 1919, but recession in the beef market began the following year and cattle sales plummeted. Cattle receipts

Clem Mason with his fiddle in 1916 at one of the Hash Knife line camps. Note brand in window. (Courtesy of Stella Hughes)

for the Hash Knife operation of Babbitt and Wyrick went from a high of $84,477 in 1918 to a mere $1,032 in 1921.[63]

Still in the business of land acquisition, the Babbitts bought a total of 74,944.77 acres on August 12, 1921, from the Aztec Land and Cattle Company. The huge tract in Navajo and Coconino counties was described as lying south of the Little Colorado River between "the middle water courses" of Clear Creek on the west and Chevelon Creek on the east.[64]

The copartnership of Charles J. Babbitt and C. E. Wyrick was reorganized on February 15, 1924, as the Wyrick Cattle Company. Included in the transfer were all Hash Knife cattle, all horses and mules branded with a Bar W, rights to all range and grazing privileges, leased land, improvements on deeded or public domain lands, and all ranch equipment.[65]

In the spring of 1925, William Babbitt shipped in a herd of cattle from western Kansas. Inspectors spotted more than a half dozen animals infected with scab, a highly infectious skin disease. They ordered the Babbitts to build dipping facilities and dip every animal on their ranches in northern Arizona, including 18,000 head on the

Clair Haight, roundup cook for the Hash Knife outfit in the 1920s. He is baking bread in a Dutch oven covered with coals. The two deep Dutch ovens suspended above the fire, usually called "meat ovens," were used for roasts or stews. (Courtesy of Stella Hughes)

C O Bar and on their Cataract Ranch between Williams and the Grand Canyon. On their Hart Ranch, another 9,000 head of Hash Knife cattle were affected. Pat Hughes, one of the Hash Knife hands at the time, vividly described what he called "scabbies": "When cattle get the scabs, little mites get under the hide and grow. In the bad stages it gets to be one big, bloody scab, right alongside the backbone and along the neck. If they ain't dipped the cattle get so poor they're on the lift [too weak to rise and have to be pulled to their feet by the tail], an' when they go down it ain't long until they're dead."[66]

The cost to the Babbitts in labor, construction of concrete dipping vats, materials, weight shrinkage, and loss of cattle was said to have been $200,000. To avoid bankruptcy, the Babbitts went outside the family in 1926 for help in the management of their faltering cattle operations by hiring a Scotsman, H. V. (Vic) Watson, away from the War Finance Corporation in Santa Fe, New Mexico. In three years he had revitalized the Arizona Loan Company, a lending institution within the family enterprises. By 1930 he was vice-president of the company and was selling off ranches that were unproductive.[67]

Because of unfavorable range conditions in 1930, the greater part of the Hash Knife herd was sold and the remaining cattle moved to the Hart range.[68] The Babbitts became sole owners of the Hash Knife Ranch on June 22, 1934, when Charles E. Wyrick sold them

Pat Hughes, rough-
string rider with the
Hash Knife outfit in the
1920s and 1930s.
(Courtesy of Stella
Hughes)

his NE ¼ of Section 26 in Navajo County to what would continue
for a time to be called the Wyrick Cattle Company.[69] Wyrick then
bought a ranch west of Heber from his brother-in-law Chet Houck.
He and his stepson, Bill Jim Wyrick, operated the ranch until the
death of the elder Wyrick on January 30, 1938.[70]

Above: Dipping Hash Knife cattle for scab in 1925. (Bill Wyrick Collection). *Right:* John G. Babbitt (1908–), boss of the Babbitt ranching division for nearly half a century. (Babbitt Brothers Trading Company)

Following Wyrick's death, an amendment to the Articles of Incorporation of the Wyrick Cattle Company was certified by the Arizona Corporation Commission on February 25, 1938, changing the name of the company to the Hash Knife Ranch, Inc.[71]

When Vic Watson left the Babbitts in December 1940, he had liquidated extensive properties but probably saved their cattle industry.[72] On July 4, 1941, the *Coconino Sun* announced the sale of the historic Hash Knife Ranch by the Babbitt Brothers Trading Company. The buyer was Fred Aja, a prominent northern Arizona sheepman, who had aspired to own the ranch since he had been a herder in the area twenty-two years earlier. The deal did not include the Hash Knife brand. The real estate transaction involved 110,000 acres in Navajo and Coconino counties. The bulk of the range averaged eight miles wide by twenty-eight miles long and included three headquarter ranches, seventeen tanks, livestock, and equipment.[73]

Once considered the scourge of the cattle industry and the reason for open warfare by cowboys of the Aztec Land and Cattle Company, sheep now grazed peacefully on former Hash Knife ranges.

Opposite top: Hash Knife cowboy Bill Jim Wyrick on the right with rope in hand. *Opposite bottom:* Hash Knife cowboys working cattle in a corral in the early 1900s. Mounted on a horse in the background is Bill Jim Wyrick. (Both photos courtesy of Stella Hughes)

Pat Hughes putting the
Hash Knife brand on a
calf in the early 1920s.
With him (*left to right*)
are Poole, Jake Miller,
and Herman Margeson.
(Courtesy of Stella
Hughes)

12

The Hash Knife Today

IME and custom have altered the size and shape of the Hash Knife brand. During the epic years of long cattle drives and district roundups, it had to be large enough, plain enough, and high enough on the animal to be discernible in mixed herds at long distances. With little or no present need for this, modern brands are somewhat reduced in size. Current designs of the Hash Knife brand in Texas and Montana are also altered from the original. The flared ends, or shoulders, of the cutting edge are now less exaggerated and the knife handles noticeably shorter.

After the Hash Knife brand and what was left of the herds in northern Arizona became a part of the livestock interests of the Babbitt Brothers Trading Company, the Aztec Land and Cattle Company continued as a landholding corporation with only limited involvement with cattle.

The Continental Land and Cattle Company in Texas was also having its troubles in the 1890s. Public comments made by John Simpson in 1887 on the questionable future of multiple cattle operations by a single company, especially those that had ranges over a thousand miles apart, were being taken seriously. In 1893 the W Ranch on the east side of the Pecos was sold to Fanning Woodyard (Woody) Johnson and his brothers.[1] In July 1897, the Arden Cattle Company of Deadwood, South Dakota, purchased the Hash Knife outfit in Montana for $300,000. Cross S herds of the purchas-

Left, a present-day Hash Knife branding iron used on the remaining part of the old Hash Knife spread in Baylor and Throckmorton counties, Texas. *Right,* a Hash Knife iron currently used in Carter County, Montana. (Photos by the author)

ing company, owned by Harris Franklin, were scheduled to be moved from their old range on the Belle Fourche River north into Hash Knife country.[2]

During a special meeting of stockholders in the offices of the Continental Land and Cattle Company at Estelline, Hall County, Texas, on March 9, 1914, a resolution was passed calling for the dissolution of the corporation. The meeting was called by Colonel William E. Hughes, owner of more than four-fifths of the total shares.[3] Small stockholders in the Mill Iron spread in the lower Panhandle then began selling their shares to the large stockholders, specifically to Colonel Hughes. On October 14, 1916, he became sole owner of the Mill Iron and all other interests of the former Continental Land and Cattle Company.[4]

At the time of his death in Dallas on June 26, 1920, John Simpson ran the Hash Knife brand on a small scale in Matagorda and Concho counties in Texas.[5] He and Royal A. Ferris, both of Dallas, had purchased 9,087 acres on March 19, 1907, on the east side of Tres Palacios Creek in Matagorda County.[6] Part of the land was surveyed and platted as a subdivision when the St. Louis, Brownsville &

Mexico Railroad, from Buckeye to Collegeport, bisected the property in 1910 and built a railroad station where an old county road crossed the rails. It became Simpsonville. When the railroad was abandoned in 1932, with it went the village of Simpsonville.[7] Deed records show that John Simpson bought 14,000 or more acres along Kickapoo Creek in Concho County on August 22, 1916, which became known as the Paint Rock Ranch.[8]

Although the historic Hash Knife brand is still registered in Arizona under the Babbitt name, its use was discontinued by the corporation around 1940. It is still a legally recognized Texas brand on a part of the old Hash Knife spread in Baylor and Throckmorton counties. In Carter County, Montana, the brand was reregistered and is presently run on a ranch northwest of Ekalaka by Fulton Castleberry, a grandson of Frank Castleberry, an old-time cowboy with the Continental Land and Cattle Company.

Cowboys of the Hash Knife ranges in the late nineteenth century were continually on the fringes of civilization and outside the normal limits of lawmen. Their brand was more than a hot iron. It represented a way of life, becoming a symbol for 1,200-mile trail drives, far-flung ranches, self-willed longhorns, hell-for-leather cowboys, and a legendary reputation that extended well beyond their ranges and into the annals of history. Never will a cattle brand stand for the likes of it again.

Notes

1. Cattlemen-Bankers with a Vision

1. G. A. Holland, assisted by Violet M. Roberts, *History of Parker County and the Double Log Cabin* (Weatherford, Texas: The Herald Publishing Co., 1937), pp. 33–38.

2. G. A. Holland, *The Man and His Monument: The Man Was J. R. Couts, His Monument the Citizens National Bank* (Weatherford, Texas: The Herald Publishing Co., 1924), pp. [3–5].

3. Ibid.

4. Holland, *History of Parker County.*

5. H[enry] Smythe, *Historical Sketches of Parker County and Weatherford, Texas* (St. Louis: Louis G. Lavat, Book and Job Printer, 1877), pp. 243–44.

6. Benjamin Capps, *The Warren Wagontrain Raid* (New York: The Dial Press, 1974), pp. 34–35.

7. Ibid.

8. Ruth Whitehead, "J. R. Couts, Gunslinging Banker," *Real West* 225, no. 187 (October 1982): 8–10, 52.

9. Smythe, *Historical Sketches.*

10. N. H. Kincaid, "John N. Simpson, Pioneer Cattleman and Financier," *The Cattleman* 33, no. 10 (March 1947): 31–32, 95–96.

11. Gus L. Ford, ed., *Texas Cattle Brands: A Catalog of the Texas Centennial Exposition Exhibit* (Dallas: C. C. Cockrell Co., 1936), p. 143.

12. *Record of Marks and Brands,* 1874–1880, Parker County, Texas, pp. 2, 7, 41. Book owned by Mary and V. Kemp, Jr., Weatherford, Texas.

2. Choosing a Brand

1. Elmo Irby, letter to Mrs. N. H. Kincaid, November 6, 1946, Naomi Kincaid Papers, Dorothy Kincaid Book, Kingsland, Texas.

2. *Record of Marks and Brands 1*, September 28, 1878, Taylor County, Texas, p. 159.

3. *Fort Griffin* (Texas) *Echo,* January 23, 1879, p. [4].

4. Emmett M. Landers, "A Short History of Taylor County" (Master's thesis, Simmons University, Abilene, Texas, August 1929), pp. 24–25.

5. Katharyn Duff, *Abilene . . . on Catclaw Creek* (Abilene, Texas: Reporter Publishing Co., 1969), pp. 32–33.

6. W. C. Holden, "The Cattlemen Get Together," *Southwest Review* 18, no. 1 (October 1932): 28–34.

7. "J. N. Simpson to Couts & Simpson, Bill of Sale," *Deed Record A,* Taylor County, Texas, March 16, 1877, pp. 112–13.

8. "Matters by Mail (Weatherford)," *Dallas* (Texas) *Daily Herald,* July 4, 1880, p. 5.

9. Bene, "Extension of the Texas and P," *Galveston* (Texas) *Daily News,* September 9, 1880, p. 4.

10. "Here Comes the T & P, Riding over the Prairie-o," *Abilene* (Texas) *Reporter-News,* Centennial Edition, March 15, 1981, p. 10.

11. *Deed Record 14,* December 18, 1880, Taylor County, Texas, pp. 13–15.

12. Naomi Kincaid, "The Founding of Abilene, the 'Future Great' of the Texas and Pacific Railway," *West Texas Historical Association Year Book* 22 (October 1946): 15–26.

13. Virginia H. Taylor, *The Franco-Texan Land Company* (Austin: University of Texas Press, 1969), pp. 187–89.

14. *Blind Asylum Land,* files 1726, 1727, 1728, 1729, Taylor County, Texas, surveyed July 9, 1879, General Land Office, Austin.

15. "Stock Notes," *Fort Griffin* (Texas) *Echo,* October 23, 1880, p. [2].

16. "Extensive Purchase of Cattle—Expecting the Normal School, Etc.," *Galveston* (Texas) *Daily News,* January 27, 1881, p. 1.

17. *Fort Griffin* (Texas) *Echo,* January 29, 1881, p. [3].

18. *Deed Record D,* Taylor County, Texas, July 6, 1881, pp. 7–16.

3. The Trans-Pecos Range

1. *Record of Marks and Brands 1,* registered November 26, 1881, Pecos County, Texas, p. 5.

2. "John Simpson, Powerhouse in Banking, Ranch Circles," *Abilene* (Texas) *Reporter-News,* April 8, 1956, p. 7-E.

3. A. P. (Ott) Black, *The End of the Long Horn Trail* (Selfridge, N.D.: The Selfridge Journal, 1936), pp. 13–14.

4. Gus L. Ford, ed., *Texas Cattle Brands: A Catalog of the Texas Centennial Exposition Exhibit* (Dallas: C. C. Cockrell Co., 1936), p. 143.

5. Toyah Historical and Centennial Committee, *Toyah Taproots: A Memory Book of Those Who Put Down Their Roots in Toyah* (Austin: Nortex Press, 1984), pp. 79–85.

6. "The Texas & Pacific," *Dallas* (Texas) *Weekly Herald,* October 13, 1881, p. 7.

7. Ibid.

8. Alton Hughes, *Pecos: A History of the Pioneer West* (Seagraves, Texas: Pioneer Book Pub., 1978), pp. 270–71.

9. Ibid.

10. Ibid.

11. Gunnar Brune, *Springs of Texas* (Fort Worth: Branch Smith, Inc., 1981), p. 148.

12. John D. Alexander, "The Rustler Hills," *Old West* (Spring 1982): 6–15.

13. Ford, *Texas Cattle Brands.*

14. "Pioneer 'Hash Knife' Boss Visits Pecos," *Pecos* (Texas) *Enterprise and Gusher,* July 10, 1931, pp. 1, 10.

15. "Statement of Mrs. A. T. Windham of Pecos, Texas," n.d., Biographical File, Eugene C. Barker Texas History Center, University of Texas, Austin.

16. Arthur Chapman, "Rodeo Dollars," *World's Work* 60, no. 7 (July 1931): 28–30.

17. "Statement of Mrs. A. T. Windham of Pecos, Texas."

18. "Petition of Citizens of Upper Pecos Valley asking to be attached to Reeves County," *Memorials and Petitions,* Tom Green County, Texas, file box no. 90, no. 123, letter no. T, 1885, Texas State Library, Archives Division, Austin.

19. *Chattel Mortgages Record 1,* Reeves County, Texas, April 30, 1885, p. 1-1.

20. Ford, *Texas Cattle Brands.*

21. "Rendered for Taxation by the Owners or Agents thereof, for the Year 1886," *Tax Roll, 1886–87,* Tom Green County, Texas, form B, p. 11-11.

22. Chuck Parsons, *Clay Allison: Portrait of a Shootist* (Seagraves, Texas: Pioneer Book Pub., 1983), pp. 54–55, 84–85.

23. *Record of Marks and Brands 1,* registered March 11, 1889, Reeves County, Texas, p. 20.

4. Between the Forks of the Brazos

1. *Marks & Brands 1,* registered January 23, 1882, Baylor County, Texas, p. 141.

2. [Don] James, "Milletts Bigger Than State; Couldn't Block Civilization," in *Salt Pork to Sirloins: The History of Baylor County from 1878 to Present,* by the Baylor County Historical Survey Committee (Wichita Falls, Texas: Nortex Press, 1977), 2: 14–15.

3. "Big Sale" [newspaper clipping], *Capt. Millett's Scrapbook,* n.d., p. 19, Ellsworth County Historical Museum, Ellsworth, Kansas.

4. "The Milletts," *Baylor County Pioneer Brands* [scrapbook], compiled by the Pierian Club of Baylor County, 1964–65, Baylor County Free Library, Seymour, Texas.

5. Pauline Durrett Robertson and R. L. Robertson, *Cowman's Country: Fifty Frontier Ranches in the Texas Panhandle* (Amarillo, Texas: Paramount Publishing Co., 1981), pp. 120–21.

6. "Charter of the 'Continental Cattle Company,'" filed in Department of

State, May 16 AD 1882, no. 1596, T. H. Bowman, secretary of state, Austin, Texas.

7. *Deed Record 3*, Baylor County, Texas, June 20, 1882, pp. 111–15.

8. Floyd Benjamin Streeter, "Longhorns–Shorthorns, the Life and Times of Captain Eugene Bartlett Millett, a Cattleman of the Old West," typescript, ca. 1955, pp. 94–95, Ellsworth County Historical Museum, Ellsworth, Kansas.

9. "Pioneer of the West," *Ellsworth* (Kansas) *Messenger*, February 24, 1916, p. 7.

10. Floyd Benjamin Streeter, "Famous Cattle Drives," *The Cattleman* 34, no. 8 (January 1948): 130, 132–33.

11. Floyd Benjamin Streeter, "The Millett Cattle Ranch in Baylor County, Texas," *Panhandle-Plains Historical Review* 22 (1949): 65–83.

12. A. P. (Ott) Black, *The End of the Long Horn Trail* (Selfridge, N.D.: The Selfridge Journal, 1936), pp. 10–15.

13. "Pioneer of the West," *Ellsworth* (Kansas) *Messenger*, March 9, 1916, p. 7.

14. Black, *The End of the Long Horn Trail*.

15. J. R. Webb, "Henry Herron, Pioneer and Peace Officer during Fort Griffin Days," *West Texas Historical Association Year Book* 20 (October 1944): 21–50.

16. Streeter, "The Millett Cattle Ranch."

17. "The Milletts."

18. "Charter of the Continental Land and Cattle Company," filed in Department of State, Jany. 30 AD 1884, no. 2266, J. W. Baines, Secretary of State, Austin, Texas.

19. "John Simpson, Powerhouse in Banking, Ranch Circles," *Abilene* (Texas) *News-Reporter*, April 1, 1956, p. 7-E.

20. N. H. Kincaid, "John N. Simpson, Pioneer Cattleman and Financier," *The Cattleman* 33, no. 10 (March 1947): 31–32, 95–96.

21. Jettie Howe Russell, "First Hashknife Hdqr.," in *Latchstrings: A Cross-Section of Baylor County Homes*, by the Baylor County Historical Society (Dallas: Taylor Publishing Co., 1986), pp. 11–12.

22. Virginia Browder, *Hall County Heritage Trails, 1890–1980* (Canyon, Texas: Staked Plains Press, 1982), 1: 20–21; 60–61.

23. Kincaid, "John N. Simpson."

24. "T. C. Irby, Sr." [obituary], *Baylor County Banner* (Seymour, Texas), September 28, 1939, p. 7.

25. *Deed Record 21*, Baylor County, Texas, May 12, 1899, pp. 430–32.

26. Russell, "First Hashknife Hdqr."

5. A New Range 1,200 Miles North

1. *Brand Records of the Territory of Montana*, 1905 series, p. 141, Recorder of Marks and Brands, Department of Livestock, Helena.

2. *Brand Book of the Montana Stock Growers' Association for 1885 and 1886* (Helena: Montana Stock Growers' Association, 1885), p. 55.

3. *Brand Records of the Territory of Montana.*

4. Robert H. Fletcher, *Free Grass to Fences: The Montana Cattle Range Story* (New York: University Publishing, Inc., 1960), p. 53.

5. "Stock Losses in Montana," *Weekly Yellowstone Journal* (Miles City, Montana), January 10, 1885, p. [4].

6. B. M. Renshaw, in collaboration with H. B. Albert, "Hash Knife and Mill Iron Ranches," in *Shifting Scenes: A History of Carter County, Montana* (Ekalaka, Mont.: Carter Geological Society; Billings, Mont.: Artcraft Printers, 1978), 1: 323–26.

7. John O. Bye, *Back Trailing in the Heart of the Short-Grass Country* (Everett, Wash.: Alexander Printing Co., 1956), pp. 17–23.

8. Hermann Hagedorn, *Roosevelt in the Bad Lands* (Boston and New York: Houghton Mifflin Co., 1921), pp. 139–47.

9. A. P. (Ott) Black, *The End of the Long Horn Trail* (Selfridge, N.D.: The Selfridge Journal, 1936), pp. 16–17.

10. "Exterminating a Gang of Horse-Thieves," *Literary Digest* 42, no. 10, whole no. 1090 (March 11, 1911): 481–83.

11. "The Little Missouri—A Terrible Fight with Horse Thieves," *Black Hills Times* (Deadwood, Dakota), February 16, 1884, p. [4].

12. Doug Engebretson, "The George Axelby Gang and 'The Stoneville Battle,'" *Real West* 26, no. 190 (April 1983): 22–27, 39.

13. Annie D. Tallent, *The Black Hills; or, The Last Hunting Ground of the Dakotahs* (St. Louis: Nixon-Jones Printing Co., 1899), pp. 560–65.

14. Engebretson, "The George Axelby Gang."

15. Bye, *Back Trailing.*

16. Orville Speelman, "Biographical Sketch of FRANK CASTLEBERRY," *WPA Livestock Study,* Carter County, Montana, typescript from MF 250, reel 16, January 8, 1940, Montana Historical Society, Helena.

17. John Snyder, "The Wickedest Town in the West," *Denver Post Empire Magazine,* August 2, 1959, pp. 10–13.

18. Renshaw, "Hash Knife and Mill Iron Ranches."

19. B. M. Beverly, letter to D. M. Frost, *Globe Live Stock Journal* (Dodge City, Kansas), June 15, 1886, p. 4.

20. "Records kept by Mr. C. H. Marselus at Trail City on Ark. River, just over line in Colo—spring of 1886," Pickett Collection, Western History Collections, Norlin Library, University of Colorado, Boulder.

21. J. R. Webb, "Chapters from the Frontier Life of Phin W. Reynolds," *West Texas Historical Association Year Book* 21 (October 1945): 110–43.

22. Black, *The End of the Long Horn Trail,* pp. 14–15.

23. *Stock Growers' Journal* (Miles City, Montana), July 31, 1886, quoted in Renshaw, "Hash Knife and Mill Iron Ranches."

24. Bye, *Back Trailing,* pp. 19–20.

25. Hagedorn, *Roosevelt in the Bad Lands,* p. 47.

26. Black, *The End of the Long Horn Trail,* pp. 27–29.

27. Ibid.

28. Ibid.

29. Milton F. Ayres, "Milliron/Hash Knife Company—Continental Cattle Company," *WPA Livestock Study*, Custer County, Montana, typescript from MF 250, reel 18, November 13, 1939, Montana Historical Society, Helena.

30. Dick Schaus, "Pioneers: Barnett Stiles," *Arizona Cattlelog* 13, no. 6 (February 1958): 10–14.

31. *Stock Growers' Journal* (Miles City, Montana), June 11, 1887, quoted in Renshaw, "Hash Knife and Mill Iron Ranches."

6. The Hash Knife Outfit in the Arizona Territory

1. Brand and Mark of Aztec Cattle Company, *Marks & Brands 2*, filed June 2, 1885, Apache County, A.T., p. 123.

2. *St. Johns* (Arizona) *Herald*, June 11, 1885, p. 4.

3. Stock Brand, Aztec Land & Cattle Co., *Marks & Brands 3*, dated August 22, 1885, Yavapai County, A.T., p. 41.

4. James Cox, *Historical and Biographical Record of the Cattle Industry and the Cattlemen of Texas and Adjacent Territory* (St. Louis, Mo.: Woodward & Tiernan Printing Co., 1894), pp. 64–65.

5. Lieut. A. W. Whipple, "Report of Explorations and Surveys to Ascertain the Most Practical and Economical Route for a Railroad from the Mississippi River to the Pacific Ocean (1852–4)," *House of Representatives Executive Document 91*, vol. 3, pt. 1, 33d Cong., 2d sess. (Washington: A. O. P. Nicholson, 1856), pp. 71–84.

6. William S. Greever, *Arid Domain: The Santa Fe Railway and Its Western Land Grant* (Palo Alto, Calif.: Stanford University Press, 1954), pp. 1–18, 46.

7. Ross L. Muir and Carl J. White, *Over the Long Term . . . the Story of J. & W. Seligman & Co.* (New York: J. & W. Seligman & Co., 1964), pp. 107–11.

8. "The 'Aztec' Company's Rights—Letter of Seligman & Seligman, of New York, to C. L. Gutterman, of Apache County," *Apache County Critic* (Holbrook, Arizona), June 3, 1886, p. 1.

9. "With a Capital of a Million," *New York Times*, January 4, 1885, p. 1.

10. Contract of Sale between the Atlantic and Pacific Railroad Company and the Aztec Land and Cattle Company, Limited, *Agreements and Leases 2*, February 3, 1886, Apache County, A.T., pp. 94–105.

11. "Local News," *St. Johns* (Arizona) *Herald*, June 18, 1885, p. 3.

12. Geo. H. Tinker, *A Land of Sunshine: Flagstaff and Its Surroundings* (Flagstaff: Arizona Champion Print, 1887), pp. 24–25.

13. The Aztec Land and Cattle Company and Henry Warren /To/ The Continental Land and Cattle Co. and E. J. Simpson, *Mortgages 2*, filed March 26, 1886, Apache County, A.T., pp. 145–53.

14. Gus L. Ford, ed., *Texas Cattle Brands: A Catalog of the Texas Centennial Exposition Exhibit* (Dallas: Clyde C. Cockrell Co., 1936), p. 143.

15. Alton Hughes, *Pecos: A History of the Pioneer West* (Seagraves, Tex.: Pioneer Book Pub., 1978), 270–71.

16. "Local News," *St. Johns* (Arizona) *Herald*, May 21, 1885, p. 3.

17. Ibid., August 6, 1885, p. 3.

18. Chuck King, "Riding the Rimrock—Aztec Land and Cattle Company," *Western Horseman* 47, no. 8 (August 1982): 12, 14.

19. "Metropolitan Mention," *Morning Journal* (Albuquerque, New Mexico), January 1, 1886, p. 5.

20. Jo Johnson, "The Hash Knife Outfit," *Arizona Highways* 32, no. 6 (June 1956): 2–7, 38–39.

21. "Territorial Stock Notes," *Hoof and Horn* (Prescott, Arizona), May 20, 1886, p. 6.

22. "Cattle Movements," *Daily News* (El Paso, Texas), June 19, 1886, p. 2.

23. Toyah Historical and Centennial Committee, *Toyah Taproots: A Memory Book of Those Who Put Down Their Roots in Toyah* (Austin, Tex.: Nortex Press, 1984), pp. 83–85.

24. Charles S. Peterson, *Take Up Your Mission: Mormon Colonizing along the Little Colorado River* (Tucson: University of Arizona Press, 1973), p. 169.

25. Richard J. Morrisy, "The Early Range Cattle Industry in Arizona," *Agricultural History* 24 (July 1950): 151–56.

26. Greever, *Arid Domain*, pp. 46–47.

27. Will C. Barnes, "Cowpunching Forty Years Ago," *Weekly Market Report and News Letter,* Arizona Cattle Growers' Association, Phoenix, no. 8 (March 10, 1931): 1–4.

28. Oren Arnold and John P. Hale, *Hot Irons: Heraldry of the Range* (New York: Macmillan Co., 1940), pp. 141–43.

29. Ibid.

30. Johnson, "The Hash Knife Outfit."

31. "Statement of Lucien Creswell," October 19, 1935, Flagstaff, Arizona, Gladwell Richardson Collection, Special Collections Library, Northern Arizona University, Flagstaff, pp. 13–17.

32. Ibid.

33. "Statement of Jim Pierce," n.d., Gladwell Richardson Collection, pp. 1–4.

34. Jo Baéza, "The Hash Knife Outfit," *Persimmon Hill* 8, no. 2 (Spring 1978): 60–69.

35. Will C. Barnes, *Apaches & Longhorns: The Reminiscences of Will C. Barnes* (Los Angeles: Ward Ritchie Press, 1941), pp. 127–29.

36. "The 'Aztec' Company's Rights—Letter of Seligman & Seligman, of New York, to C. L. Gutterson, of Apache County."

37. "Territorial Stock Notes," *St. Johns* (Arizona) *Herald,* June 10, 1886, p. 1.

38. Albert F. Potter, "A Brief History of the Cattle Business in Apache County, Arizona," MS (1901), Special Collections, University of Arizona Library, Tucson, pp. 1–6.

39. Bert Haskett, "Early History of the Cattle Industry in Arizona," *Arizona Historical Review* 6, no. 4 (October 1935): 3–42.

40. Baéza, "The Hash Knife Outfit."

41. James W. LeSueur, "Trouble with the Hash Knife Cattle Company" (n.d.), James W. LeSueur Papers, MS 433, Arizona Historical Society, Tucson.

42. Will C. Barnes, "A Mistake Brand Adopted," *St. Johns* (Arizona) *Herald*, December 2, 1886, p. 3.

43. Baéza, "The Hash Knife Outfit."

44. Roscoe G. Willson, "Brand-Doctoring Artists Led a Touch-and-Go Life," *Arizona Days & Ways* (Arizona Republic Magazine), Phoenix, July 15, 1962, pp. 22–23.

45. Barnes, *Apaches & Longhorns*, pp. 136–43.

46. "Local Items," *St. Johns* (Arizona) *Herald*, April 14, 1887, p. 3.

47. Barnes, *Apaches & Longhorns*.

48. LeSueur, "Trouble with the Hash Knife Cattle Company."

49. Will C. Barnes, "The Pleasant Valley War of 1887: Its Genesis, History and Necrology," *Arizona Historical Review* 4, no. 4 (January 1932): 23–40.

50. Ibid.

51. "Local News," *St. Johns* (Arizona) *Herald*, August 18, 1887, p. 3.

52. B. F. Irby, "Rodeo Notice," ibid.

53. Ibid.

54. Barnes, *Apaches & Longhorns*, pp. 132–35.

55. Robin May, *History of the American West* (New York: Exeter Books, 1984), p. 157.

56. Earle R. Forrest, *Arizona's Dark and Bloody Ground*, rev. ed. (Caldwell, Idaho: Caxton Printers, Ltd., 1950), pp. 109–53.

57. "Winslow Pickings," *St. Johns* (Arizona) *Herald*, December 16, 1887, p. 3.

58. Don Dedera, *A Little War of Our Own: The Pleasant Valley Feud Revisited* (Flagstaff, Ariz.: Northland Press, 1988), p. 1.

59. Forrest, *Arizona's Dark and Bloody Ground*, pp. 193–219.

60. Ibid.

61. "The Pleasant Valley Lynching," *Arizona Weekly Journal-Miner* (Prescott), August 22, 1888, p. 1.

62. Oren, "Our Holbrook Letter," *Apache Review* (St. Johns, Arizona), June 13, 1888, p. 3.

63. Morrisy, "The Early Range Cattle Industry in Arizona."

64. Uncle Zek, "Holbrooklets," *Apache Review* (St. Johns, Arizona), June 6, 1888, p. 3.

65. *Apache Review* (St. Johns, Arizona), August 29, 1888, p. 3.

66. "Holbrook Items," ibid., August 22, 1888, p. 3.

67. Morrisy, "The Early Range Cattle Industry in Arizona."

68. "Statement of Jim Pierce."

69. "Statement of Lucien Creswell," pp. 13–15.

70. "Statement of Jim Pierce."

71. William Sparks, "The Canyon Diablo Train Robbery and Capture of the Robbers by Buckey O'Neal [sic] as Told by Dan Harvick, One of the Robbers, to William Sparks," in *The Apache Kid: A Bear Fight and Other True Stories of the Old West* by William Sparks (Los Angeles: Skelton Publishing Co., 1926), pp. 144–63.

72. "A Bold Robbery," *Arizona Weekly Champion* (Flagstaff), March 23, 1889, p. 3.

73. Gladwell Richardson, *Two Guns, Arizona* (Santa Fe: Press of the Territorian, 1968), pp. 15–17.

74. Sparks, "The Canyon Diablo Train Robbery."

75. "Statement of William 'Bill' Rhoden [Roden]," August 12, 1931, Gladwell Richardson Collection, Special Collections Library, Northern Arizona University, Flagstaff. pp. 1–14.

76. Sparks, "The Canyon Diablo Train Robbery."

77. "Personnel of the Fifteenth," *Phoenix* (Arizona) *Daily Herald*, February 15, 1889, p. 2.

78. Elizabeth Simpson, letter to Mrs. Naomi Kincaid, October 30, 1946, Naomi Kincaid Papers, Dorothy Kincaid Book, Kingsland, Texas.

79. "Local News," *St. Johns* (Arizona) *Herald*, June 9, 1887, p. 3.

80. "The Court at St. Johns," *Arizona Weekly Champion* (Flagstaff), October 1, 1887, p. 3.

81. "Local News," *St. Johns* (Arizona) *Herald*, September 22, 1887, p. 3.

82. Stock Brand, Aztec Land & Cattle Co., *Record of Marks & Brands 1*, dated October 12, 1895, Coconino County, A.T., p. 273.

83. Stock Brand, Yavapai County, A.T.

84. Brand and Earmarks, Aztec Land & Cattle Co., *Marks & Brands 1*, recorded February 18, 1897, Navajo County, A.T., p. 35.

85. Barnes, *Apaches & Longhorns*, p. 132.

86. Dick Schaus, "Pioneers: Barnett Stiles," *Arizona Cattlelog* 13, no. 6 (February 1958): 10–14.

87. Dane Coolidge, *Fighting Men of the West* (New York: E. P. Dutton & Co., 1932), pp. 124–25, 247–57.

88. Frazier Hunt, *Cap Mossman, Last of the Great Cowmen* (New York: Hastings House, 1951), pp. 83–84.

89. Ibid., pp. 85–92.

90. Ibid., p.96.

91. Bill of Sale, Waters Cattle Company to Aztec Land and Cattle Company, *Miscellaneous Documents 3*, dated July 20, 1896, Apache County, A.T., p. 147.

92. Schaus, "Pioneers: Barnett Stiles."

93. Hunt, *Cap Mossman*, pp. 110–11.

94. Ibid., pp. 112–14.

95. Ibid., pp. 126–29.

96. Ibid., pp. 134–35.

97. Ibid., pp. 129–33.

98. Schaus, "Pioneers: Barnett Stiles."

99. "Local and Personal," *Holbrook* (Arizona) *Argus*, November 11, 1899, p. 5.

100. "The Local Field," ibid., September 29, 1900, p. 1.

101. Mulford Winsor, "The Arizona Rangers," *Our Sheriff and Police Journal* 31, no. 6 (June 1936): 49–61.

7. Rhyming Robber of the Hash Knife

1. "Holbrook Locals," *St. Johns* (Arizona) *Herald,* June 7, 1888, p. 3.

2. *Apache Review* (St. Johns, Arizona), June 6, 1888, p. 3.

3. Platt Cline, "Pistol Packin' Poet," *Scenic Southwest* 19, no. 7 (July 1947): 3, 6, 22–26.

4. Harold C. Wayte, Jr., "A History of Holbrook and the Little Colorado River Country (1540–1962)," Master's thesis, 1962, University of Arizona, Tucson, pp. 192–200.

5. *Tombstone* (Arizona) *Epitaph,* January 21, 1888, p. [3], January 28, 1888, p. [3].

6. Cline, "Pistol Packin' Poet."

7. "Poetry Composed by the Desperado, R. W. McNail [sic]," *St. Johns* (Arizona) *Herald,* April 25, 1889, p. 3.

8. Wayte, "A History of Holbrook."

9. *Apache Review* (St. Johns, Arizona), August 15, 1888, p. 3.

10. William French, *Some Recollections of a Western Ranchman, New Mexico, 1883–1899* (London: Methuen & Co., Ltd., 1927), pp. 153–60.

11. "Everywhere," *Arizona Champion* (Flagstaff), September 22, 1888, p. 2.

12. Wayte, "A History of Holbrook."

13. French, *Some Recollections of a Western Ranchman.*

14. Ibid.

15. "The Notorious McNail [sic] in a New Role," *St. Johns* (Arizona) *Herald,* April 25, 1889, p. 3.

16. "Local News," ibid., May 16, 1888, p. 3.

17. Cline, "Pistol Packin' Poet" (lines 19 and 24, left out of Cline, are from Wayte, "A History of Holbrook").

18. "A Full Confession," *Utah Enquirer* (Provo), September 24, 1889, p. 3; "The Train Robbers Confess," *Standard* (Ogden, Utah), September 24, 1889, p. [4].

19. "Daring Theft of $336," *Standard* (Ogden, Utah), September 8, 1889, p. [1].

20. "Cleverly Captured," ibid., September 18, 1889, p. [4].

21. "A Full Confession."

22. "The Faro Bank Robbers," *Standard* (Ogden, Utah), September 20, 1889, p. [4].

23. "Dayton Talks," ibid., September 25, 1889, p. [4].

24. *The People vs. Ed. Fisher et al.,* packet 12, September 25, 1889, First District Court, Utah County, Provo City, U.T.; "List of Prisoners in the Utah Penitentiary," *Admission Records C,* Utah State Prison, Draper, p. 63-63; "List of Prisoners in the Utah State Prison," *Admission Records D,* 1889–July 1908, Utah State Prison, Draper, p. 2-2.

25. Cline, "Pistol Packin' Poet."

26. *Half A Century 1884–1934,* editorial reprint (Holbrook, Ariz.: Holbrook Tribune-News, 1934?), p. [3].

27. Wayte, "A History of Holbrook."

28. French, *Some Recollections of a Western Ranchman*, p. 160.

8. A Song about Mose Tate

1. Will C. Barnes, "The Cowboy and His Songs," *Saturday Evening Post* 197, no. 52 (June 27, 1925): 14–15, 122, 125, 128.

2. Ibid.

3. Ibid.

4. "Lorena" [sheet music], poetry by Rev. H. D. L. Webster, music by J. P. Webster, published by H. M. Higgins, Chicago, 1857.

5. Ernest K. Emurian, *The Sweetheart of the Civil War: The True Story of the Song "Lorena"* (Natick, Mass.: W. A. Wilde Co., 1962), pp. 26, 35, 58.

6. Albert F. Potter, "How the Bucket of Blood Got Its Name," typescript, n.d., biographical file R 646 p - Roberts, Paul H., Arizona Historical Society, Tucson; "Local and Personal," *Holbrook* (Arizona) *Argus*, May 8, 1897, p. 3.

7. Barnes, "The Cowboy and His Songs."

8. Moses Robert Tate, *Resident Card*, no. 26, Arizona Pioneers' Home, Prescott.

9. "Pioneer Cowboy's Last Range Ride," *Prescott* (Arizona) *Journal-Miner*, October 8, 1918, p. 6.

10. J. Evetts Haley, *Charles Goodnight, Cowman & Plainsman* (Boston and New York: Houghton Mifflin Co., 1936), pp. 276–94.

11. Harley True Burton, *A History of the JA Ranch* (New York: Argonaut Press, Ltd., 1966), pp. 24–26.

12. Annie Dyer Nunn, "Uncle Jim Owens Visits Panhandle," *Frontier Times* 5, no. 12 (September 1928): 454–55, 495.

13. Laura V. Hamner, *Short Grass and Longhorns* (Norman: University of Oklahoma Press, 1943), pp. 160–72.

14. Tate, *Resident Card;* "Local News," *St. Johns* (Arizona) *Herald*, June 11, 1885, p. 3.

15. Rangeman, "Local News," *St. Johns Herald*, April 7, 1887, p. 3.

16. Sallie Reynolds Matthews, *Interwoven: A Pioneer Chronicle* (Houston, Texas: Anson Jones Press, 1936), pp. 174–75.

17. Will C. Barnes, "Cowpunching Forty Years Ago," *Weekly Market Report and News Letter*, Arizona Cattle Growers' Association, Phoenix, no. 8 (March 10, 1931): 1–4.

18. "Town and Vicinity," *Apache County Critic* (Holbrook, Arizona), August 27, 1887, p. 3.

19. *Marks & Brands 2*, Apache County, A.T., recorded June 25, 1888, p. 285.

20. [Arthur] Chapman, "Mose Tate," July 1925, Will Croft Barnes Collection, box 18, folder 109, Arizona Historical Society, Tucson.

21. "Pioneer Cowboy's Last Range Ride."

22. Barnes, "The Cowboy and His Songs."

23. Will C. Barnes, "Wild Cattle and a Railroad Strike," *The Cattleman* 21, no. 10 (March 1935): 23, 25, 27–30, 32–34.

24. Del Marlow, "The Evolution of the Cowboy Boot," pt. 1, *Western Horseman* 46, no. 6 (June 1981): pp. 13–16, 18–20.

25. Barnes, "Wild Cattle and a Railroad Strike."

26. "Pioneer Cowboy's Last Range Ride"; "The Local Field," *Holbrook* (Arizona) *Argus*, May 12, 1900, p. 3.

27. Tate, *Resident Card*.

9. Trouble between Cowboys and Navajos

1. Will C. Barnes, "Wild Cattle and a Railroad Strike," *The Cattleman* 21, no. 10 (March 1935): 23, 25, 27–30, 32–34.

2. Rangeman, "Local News," *St. Johns* (Arizona) *Herald*, April 7, 1887, p. 3.

3. Barnes, "Wild Cattle and a Railroad Strike."

4. Bernice Eastman Johnston, *Two Ways in the Desert: A Study of Modern Navajo-Anglo Relations* (Pasadena, Calif.: Socio-Technical Publications, 1972), pp. 95–96.

5. "The Indian Trouble," *Coconino Sun* (Flagstaff, Arizona), July 18, 1891, p. 3.

6. Ibid.; Philip Johnston, "The Bravest Man I Ever Knew," *Los Angeles Times Sunday Magazine*, June 18, 1933, pp. 3, 18.

7. Ibid.

8. Gladwell Richardson, *Two Guns, Arizona* (Santa Fe, N.M.: Press of the Territorian, 1968), pp. 17–18.

9. "Fight with Navajoes," *Coconino Sun* (Flagstaff, Arizona), November 18, 1899, p. 1; "Wm. A. Montgomery vs. Navajo Indians," *Coroner's Inquest*, No. 71, November 13, 1899, Flagstaff, Arizona.

10. "Statement of William 'Bill' Rhoden [Roden]," Flagstaff, Arizona, August 12, 1931, Gladwell Richardson Collection, Special Collections Library, Northern Arizona University, Flagstaff; "Fight with Navajoes."

11. "Montgomery vs. Navajo Indians."

12. "Local History and Biography from Interviews with Folks You Know: Walter W. Durham," *Coconino Sun* (Flagstaff, Arizona), February 22, 1929, sec. 2, pp. 1, 6.

13. "Fight with Navajoes."

14. Burton C. Mossman, letter to Mr. and Mrs. Geo. W. Hennessey, November 7, 1955, Aztec Land and Cattle Company, Mesa, Arizona.

15. J. Lee Correll, "Gun Fight at Anderson Mesa South of Winslow, Arizona," *Navajo Times* (Window Rock, Arizona), March 24, 1966, pp. 16, 23.

16. Johnston, "The Bravest Man I Ever Knew."

17. Gladwell Richardson, *Navajo Trader* (Tucson: University of Arizona Press, 1986), pp. 27–28.

18. Correll, "Gun Fight at Anderson Mesa."

19. Johnston, *Two Ways in the Desert;* "Navajo Murder Case," *Coconino Sun* (Flagstaff, Arizona), September 22, 1900, p. 9.

20. Richard E. Sloan, *Memories of an Arizona Judge* (Stanford, Calif.: Stanford University Press, 1932), pp. 196–97.

10. Sheriff Frank Wattron

1. "Frank J. Wattron," *Holbrook* (Arizona) *Argus,* June 19, 1897, p. 2.

2. Richard E. Sloan, *Memories of an Arizona Judge* (Stanford, Calif.: Stanford University Press, 1932), pp. 186–87.

3. Dane Coolidge, *Fighting Men of the West* (New York: E. P. Dutton and Co., 1932), pp. 127–29.

4. "Town and Vicinity," *Apache County Critic* (Holbrook, Arizona), August 27, 1887, p. 2.

5. Coolidge, *Fighting Men of the West;* "Town and Vicinity," *Apache County Critic* (Holbrook, Arizona), March 31, 1887, p. 3.

6. Harold C. Wayte, Jr., "A History of Holbrook and the Little Colorado River Country (1540–1962)," thesis, 1962, University of Arizona, Tucson, p. 178.

7. Coolidge, *Fighting Men of the West,* pp. 248–49; "Frank J. Wattron."

8. C. O. Anderson, letter to Mrs. [George F.] Kitt, March 29, 1934, Arizona Historical Society, Tucson.

9. "A Brutal Murder," *Holbrook* (Arizona) *Argus,* April 1, 1899, p. 5.

10. "George Smiley Executed," ibid., January 13, 1900, p. 5.

11. "A Brutal Murder."

12. Burton C. Mossman, letter to Mr. and Mrs. Geo. W. Hennessey, November 7, 1955, Aztec Land and Cattle Company, Mesa, Arizona.

13. "A Brutal Murder."

14. "Court Proceedings," *Holbrook* (Arizona) *Argus,* October 14, 1899, p. 5.

15. "Smiley's Respite," ibid., December 16, 1899.

16. Sloan, *Memories of an Arizona Judge,* p. 186.

17. Wayte, "A History of Holbrook."

18. "Smiley's Respite."

19. "A Wierd [*sic*] Invitation," *Holbrook* (Arizona) *Argus,* November 11, 1899, p. 5.

20. "Arizona Day by Day," *Arizona Republican* (Phoenix), December 4, 1899, p. 4.

21. C. O. Anderson, letter to Mrs. [George F.] Kitt.

22. "Smiley's Respite"; "Murderer Smiley—He Will Not Hang at Holbrook, A.T. Tomorrow," *Daily Citizen* (Albuquerque, N.M.), December 7, 1899, p. 3.

23. [Editorial], *Arizona Republican* (Phoenix), December 8, 1899, p. 2.

24. "Smiley's Respite."

25. Wayte, "A History of Holbrook," pp. 186–87.

26. "George Smiley Executed."

27. Burton C. Mossman, letter to Mr. and Mrs. Geo. W. Hennessey.

28. Platt Cline, "The 'Cordial' Invitation," *Scenic Southwest* 19, no. 4 (April 1947): 3, 16, 22.

11. The Babbitt Era

1. Earle R. Forrest, "The Old-Time Cow Country of Northern Arizona," *Frontier Times* 12, no. 3 (December 1934): 123–28.

2. Earle R. Forrest, "Fort Rickerson, Greatest Cattle Ranch in Southwest," *Frontier Times* 12, no. 4 (January 1935): 158–66.

3. Charles S. Peterson, "'A Mighty Brother Was Brother Lot': A Portrait of Lot Smith—Mormon Frontiersman," *Western Historical Quarterly* 1, no. 4 (October 1970): 393–414.

4. Dean Smith, "Babbitt History," MS, ca. 1965, Special Collections Library, Northern Arizona University, Flagstaff, chap. 5, pp. 2–6.

5. W. D. Hathaway, "David Babbitt Tells of Early Days in Flagstaff," *Coconino Sun* (Flagstaff, Arizona), 45th Anniversary Pioneer Edition, November 25, 1927, sec. 7, pp. 1, 5.

6. "Local Matters," *Arizona Champion* (Flagstaff), April 10, 1886, p. 3.

7. Ibid., April 24, 1886, p. 3.

8. Smith, "Babbitt History."

9. Richard G. Schaus, "William George Babbitt, 1863–1930," *Arizona Cattlelog* 14, no. 12 (August 1963): back cover, 56.

10. Frank J. Turley, "A History of Babbitt Brothers Trading Company Emphasizing Its Economic Influence on Northern Arizona, thesis, August 1939, Arizona State Teacher's College, Flagstaff, pp. 39–40.

11. Dean Smith, "The Babbitts, Arizona Cattlemen for More Than 75 Years," *Arizona Cattlelog* 21, no. 3 (November 1964): 10, 12–14, 16.

12. Smith, "Babbitt History," chap. 7, pp. 4–5.

13. James H. McClintock, *Mormon Settlement in Arizona: A Record of Peaceful Conquest of the Desert* (Phoenix, Ariz.: Manufacturing Stationers, Inc., 1921), pp. 159–60.

14. *Deed Record 7*, Coconino County, A.T., pp. 249–55.

15. *Deed Record 14*, Coconino County, A.T., pp. 543–45.

16. Turley, "A History of the Babbitt Brothers Trading Company," pp. 40–42.

17. Albert Strauss, first vice-president, Aztec Land and Cattle Company, letter to bondholders, dated January 31, 1903, Aztec Land and Cattle Company, Mesa, Arizona.

18. "George Hennessey, 95; last of Hashknife cowboys," *Arizona Republic* (Phoenix), January 18, 1973, p. D-6.

19. Ross L. Muir and Carl J. White, *Over the Long Term . . . the Story of J. & W. Seligman & Co.* (New York: J. & W. Seligman & Co., 1964), pp. 107–11.

20. Dick Schaus, "Pioneers: Barnett Stiles," *Arizona Cattlelog* 13, no. 6 (February 1958): 10–14.

21. *General Index to Deeds 1*, Coconino County, A.T., May 7, 1902, pp. 30, 774.

22. *Deed Record 3*, Navajo County, A.T., January 24, 1903, pp. 170–71.

23. Vada Carlson and Joe Rodriguez, *A Town Is Born: A Pictorial Review of Winslow, Arizona, First Fifty Years* (Winslow, Ariz.: privately printed, 1981), pp. 35–41.

24. "Statement of Lucien Creswell," October 19, 1935, Flagstaff, Arizona, Gladwell Richardson Collection, Special Collections Library, Northern Arizona University, Flagstaff, pp. 3–4.

25. Ibid.

26. Gladwell Richardson, "A Drink for the Dead," *Arizona Highways* 39, no. 6 (June 1963): 34–39.

27. "Robber Killed in Fight," *Coconino Sun* (Flagstaff, Arizona), April 15, 1905, p. 1.

28. "Testimony of C. I. Houck, Sheriff of Navajoe," coroner's inquest, Canyon Diablo, A.T., April 8, 1905.

29. "Statement of F. W. Volz," coroner's inquest, Canyon Diablo, A.T., April 8, 1905.

30. Calico Jones [Gladwell Richardson], "Dead Bandit's Last Drink," *Western Digest* 1, no. 4 (September 1969): 48–53, 87–96.

31. James R. [Jim Bob] Tinsley, "The Violent Beginnings of Canyon Diablo and Two Guns, Arizona," MS, April 1959, Arizona State College, Flagstaff, pp. 12–13.

32. James R. Jennings, *Arizona Was the West* (San Antonio, Texas: Naylor Co., [1970]), pp. 93–94.

33. "Statement of F. W. Volz."

34. Jones, "Dead Bandit's Last Drink."

35. "Verdict of Jury in the matter of the Inquisition upon the body of John Shaw, Deceased," April 8, 1905, Coconino County, A.T., filed July 1, 1905.

36. "Statement of Lucien Creswell."

37. Richardson, "A Drink for the Dead."

38. F. A. Eyman, superintendent of Arizona State Prisons, letter to Gladwell Richardson, dated March 1, 1962.

39. "Murder at Winslow," *Arizona Journal-Miner* (Prescott), October 31, 1905, p. 1.

40. Bob D. Blair, "The Murder of William Joe Giles, 1905," *Journal of Arizona History* 7, no. 1 (Spring 1966): 27–34.

41. "Pemberton and the Unlucky No. 13," *Prescott* (Arizona) *Journal-Miner*, December 4, 1906, p. 4.

42. "Slayer of Winslow Marshall Goes Unpunished," ibid., November 8, 1905, p. 3.

43. Blair, "The Murder of William Joe Giles."

44. Stella Hughes, *Hashknife Cowboy: Recollections of Mack Hughes* (Tucson: University of Arizona Press, 1984), pp. 18, 116.

45. Smith, "Babbitt History," chap. 7, pp. 8–10.

46. *Deeds 6*, Navajo County, A.T., March 16, December 20, 1910, pp. 15–16.

47. Schaus, "Pioneers: Barnett Stiles."

48. *Deeds 6*, Navajo County, A.T., December 21, 1910, pp. 17–18.

49. "Edward H. Bargman, Pioneer Stockman, Claimed by Death," *Winslow* (Arizona) *Mail*, January 24, 1947, pp. 1, 4.

50. Smith, "Babbitt History," chap. 7, pp. 15–16, and Smith, "The Babbitts"; John G. Babbitt, *The Babbitt Brothers Trading Company* (Flagstaff, Ariz.: Northland Press, 1967), p. 13.

51. Smith, "Babbitt History," chap. 7, pp. 11–12.

52. Kell M. Fox and Frederic E. Fox, "Babbitt Bros.," MS, chap. 11, Babbitt Brothers Trading Company, Flagstaff, Arizona, [1940].

53. Ibid.

54. Hughes, *Hashknife Cowboy*, pp. 12–14.

55. "Investigation of Marley Case," *Winslow* (Arizona) *Mail*, March 11, 1911, p. 1.

56. *Judgment—The State of Arizona vs. J. W. Marley, R. S. Marley, A. C. Marley, G. D. Marley*, case no. 172, October 29, 1912, Navajo County, Arizona.

57. "Marley Case up for Trial," *Winslow* (Arizona) *Mail*, October 26, 1912, p. 1.

58. Fox and Fox, "Babbitt Bros."

59. "The Marley Case Has Been Settled after Three Years; Gladsome News," *Winslow* (Arizona) *Mail*, July 25, 1914, p. 1.

60. Fox and Fox, "Babbitt Bros."

61. Smith, "Babbitt History."

62. *Deeds 7*, Navajo County, Arizona, March 11, 14, 23, 1914, pp. 143–47.

63. Smith, "Babbitt History," chap. 7, p. 16.

64. *Deed Book 12*, Navajo County, Arizona, August 12, 1921, pp. 628–32.

65. "Bill of Sale," Babbitt and Wyrick to Wyrick Cattle Company, February 15, 1924, Babbitt Brothers Trading Company, Flagstaff, Arizona.

66. Hughes, *Hashknife Cowboy*, pp. 110–14.

67. Marshall Trimble, *C O Bar: Bill Owen Depicts the Historic Babbitt Ranch* (Flagstaff, Ariz.: Northland Press, 1982), pp. 40, 44.

68. Turley, "A History of Babbitt Brothers Trading Company," pp. 44–45.

69. *Record of Deeds 25*, Navajo County, Arizona, June 22, 1934, p. 417.

70. "Pioneer Sheep and Cattleman of North Dead," *Winslow* (Arizona) *Mail*, February 4, 1938, pp. 1, 7.

71. *Amendment of Articles of Incorporation of Wyrick Cattle Company*, February 25, 1938, Arizona Corporation Commission, Phoenix.

72. Trimble, *C O Bar.*

73. "Old Historic Hashknife Ranch Sold," *Coconino Sun* (Flagstaff, Arizona), July 4, 1941, p. 1.

12. The Hash Knife Today

1. Robert W. Dunn, "The History of Loving County, Texas," *West Texas Historical Association Year Book* 24 (October 1948): 97–119.

2. "A $300,000 Cattle Sale," *Stock Growers' Journal* (Miles City, Montana), July 31, 1897, p. 5.

3. "Certificate of Dissolution," Continental Land & Cattle Company, April 27, 1914, pp. 1–5, Office of the Secretary of State, Austin.

4. *Deeds 30*, Hall County, Texas, October 14, 1916, p. 346.

5. Sloan Simpson, letter to Mrs. Naomi Kincaid, September 30, 1946, Naomi Kincaid Papers, Dorothy Kincaid Book, Kingsland, Texas.

6. *Deed and Land Records 19*, Matagorda County, Texas, March 19, 1907, pp. 181–86.

7. Herbert W. Henry, "Simpsonville and Tintop Communities," *Historic Matagorda County* (Houston: D. Armstrong Co., 1986), 1: 401–2.

8. *Deed Record 2*, Concho County, Texas, August 22, 1916, pp. 512–15.

Index